Your Mark On The World

Stories of service that show us how to give more with a purpose
without giving up what's most important.

Devin D. Thorpe

Your Mark On The World

Stories of service that show us how to give more with a purpose without giving up what's most important.

ISBN: 1478239697

ISBN-13: 978-1478239697

Dedication

Henry,

Thank you for being such a good example for me — and everyone else!

Best Wishes,

Acknowledgements

This book has been a joy to write largely because I have received so much support from virtually everyone that has come into contact with the project over the past six months. I am extraordinarily grateful to the people who are mentioned in the book as they gave so generously of their time to become part of the story. There are many people, like Julie and David Monson, Rainer and Trix Dahl, Traci Monson, Cindy England, Paul Joseph, Wendy Powell, Debbie Hill, Sue Krupa Gray, Katy Holt-Larsen, and Ryan Anthony who helped me find the people I've written about in the book. Some early readers that provided great feedback and helped to improve the book dramatically include Trix Dahl, Paul Joseph and Mark Morrison. Matt and CarrieAnn Madden were gracious hosts to their new home country of Cambodia during my visit there; CarrieAnn even spent a day in an orphanage with me.

John T. Child created a cover for the book that challenged me to write a book worthy of its cover. Natalie Child did an exceptional job of copyediting.

Gail Thorpe, my wife, has made the greatest sacrifices for this book, not only allowing me time to write, but providing invaluable feedback as the first reviewer, always complimenting the work so that I'd have the courage to show it to someone who would then tell me how to fix it. She's also given me the incomparable gift of time to promote the book, ensuring that the book is not only written, but also read.

Despite the help I've received from so many people, any errors that remain in the text are my responsibility alone.

The following people provided financial support for the publication of this book on behalf of the cause listed; I am extraordinarily grateful to them.

Supporters over $100:

Jami Hunsaker
Koins for Kenya
www.koinsforkenya.org
Koins for Kenya builds a bridge across the world to offer educational opportunities where there are none. Rural Africans long for a chance to overcome the abject poverty that has held them hostage for generations. Since 2003 KFK has provided ways for caring Americans to actively engage with rural Kenyans.

Rainer and Trix Dahl
The Road Home
www.theroadhome.org
The Road Home is a private non-profit social service agency that assists individuals and families experiencing homelessness in Salt Lake County and along the Wasatch Front. Our mission is to help people step out of homelessness and back into our community.

Joshua and Jacob Chow
Brigham Young University
byu.edu
The mission of Brigham Young University–founded, supported, and guided by The Church of Jesus Christ of Latter-day Saints–is to assist individuals in their quest for perfection and eternal life.

Supporters over $50:

Becky Mitchell
Sunshine Project
www.the-sunshine-project.org
Students and faculty at Nanjing University in China formed the Sunshine Project, building on a ten year track record, to provide volunteers and financial support to the Gao Chuan Special School, a school for deaf and intellectually challenged students.

Colin Robinson
Boy Scouts of America
www.scouting.org
The Boy Scouts of America provides a program for young people that builds character, trains them in the responsibilities of participating citizenship, and develops personal fitness.

David Monson
Starfish Foster Home
http://www.thestarfishfosterhome.org
Starfish Foster Home, located in Xi'an, China, is a home to about 30-35 babies – children from local orphanages who are in need of specific medical care.

Michele French
The More Project
www.themoreproject.org
I have received "more" than I could ever give, from having had the privilege of serving the women and children of More Project, in Brazil. Each time that I return from the Favelas, I, myself return with more faith, more compassion, more gratitude and a greater sense of life's purpose. My heart and soul are well fed there.

Susan Montgomory
Sunshine Project
www.the-sunshine-project.org
Students and faculty at Nanjing University in China formed the Sunshine Project, building on a ten year track record, to provide volunteers and financial support to the Gao Chuan Special School, a school for deaf and intellectually challenged students.

Supporters over $20:

Beth Smith Low
Together Strong, a testicular cancer awareness organization
www.togetherstrongagainsttc.org

Bricker Thorpe
Juvenile Diabetes Research Foundation
www.jdrf.org

Bridgett Thorpe
Juvenile Diabetes Research Foundation
www.jdrf.org

Cheryl Conner
Courage Above Mountains
www.fishbowlinventory.com/cam-foundation

Christian Thorpe
Make a Wish Foundation
www.wish.org

John and Natalie Child
Susan G. Komen for the Cure
ww5.komen.org

Juliet Jackson
Big Brothers Big Sisters
www.bbbs.org

Paul Harold
Any Good Cause*

Russ Isaacson
Southwest Commonwealth School

Other Supporters:

Chris Van Tassell
Feng Tai Orphanage

Alex Budak
StartSomeGood

Brandon Stoddard
Any Good Cause*

Dayton Thorpe
Susan G. Komen for the Cure

Julie B Waters
Helping Hands for Haiti

Kirby Trumbo
Any Good Cause*

Lance Soffe
Any Good Cause*

Marty Kibiloski
One World Running

Michael Elifritz
Any Good Cause*

Paul Joseph
Caring Voice Coalition

Susan Bishop
Any Good Cause*

Tiffany Black
Any Good Cause*

Jason Mitchell
Sunshine Project

Michael Cragun
Any Good Cause*

Wendy Powell
Sunshine Project

Mark and Maryann Morrison
Grameen Foundation

Paula Ferrell
Any Good Cause*

*These supporters did not designate specific causes for their support.

Disclaimer

Neither the author nor any other person associated with this book may be held liable for any damages that may result from following the counsel in this book. No single book of financial advice can be used as a substitute for professional, personalized financial advice. Readers are encouraged to seek financial advice from qualified professionals, including licensed Investment advisors, stock brokers, accountants, insurance agents, attorneys and other qualified individuals.

About the Author

I am merely the sum of my parts.

Let's be clear about one thing right now. I am not Mother Teresa or Bill Gates. I aspire to be like them in many ways, but if you measure me by the standards they set, I will appear very small indeed.

While living in China for the last year, I've had the opportunity to think deeply about who I am and who I want to be. The past year has also given me an opportunity to see the world and its problems through a new lens. The most important thing I've seen is that there are huge problems in the world to which many wonderful people—people far greater than I—have devoted themselves to solving.

So my proposed contribution to the effort, is to help more people do more good in the world by writing about how we can all do more.

Now, you may appropriately ask what qualifies me to write this book in the first place. Let me try to address that in a way that will give you sufficient comfort to keep reading this book, rather than dismissing its contents as the mindless musings of mediocre man.

In China, I have been working as a professor of Business, principally at South China University of Technology in Guangzhou in the southern province of Guangdong about two hours from Hong Kong.

Previously, I worked as the Chief Financial Officer of a global company called MonaVie (#18 on the 2009 Inc. 500 with $834 million in revenue). This job gave me the opportunity to do business in countries all around the world—I'll never forget visiting Israel during the war in January of 2010.

Prior to that I had the opportunity to work for Utah Governor Jon Huntsman in the Utah State Government for an agency called USTAR, where I quickly learned I was not cut out to be a bureaucrat.

For the seven years before that, I owned and operated a boutique investment bank creatively named Thorpe Capital. We operated an investment advisory business as a part of the company for several years.

Though I am no longer licensed to deal in securities, at one point I had, I believe, six such licenses authorizing me to do all sorts of work in the securities arena, including running a firm, acting as the chief regulatory officer and functioning as the chief operations and finance officer.

Previously, I served as the treasurer for a then Nasdaq-listed (now NYSE-listed) company called USANA Health Sciences, Inc. (USNA) that also conducted business globally.

Going back even farther, I operated a mortgage brokerage. And before that, I worked on Capitol Hill, on the staff of the Senate Banking Committee, where I got a birds-eye view of financial markets and their regulation—what an education!

Speaking of education, I earned an MBA at Cornell's Johnson Graduate School of Management after completing a B.S. degree in finance at the University of Utah.

So there you have it, a lengthy career spent entirely in finance, which explains why I approach the solution to the world's great problems largely from a financial viewpoint.

Table of Contents

Preface

An Eleven-year-old's Promise

Saturday, June 5, 1976, was a beautiful, sunny day in Eastern Idaho. People were going about their mostly agricultural business as usual. Little did they know that a silent, unannounced disaster awaited them.

Four years earlier, the U.S. Government had begun construction on a large, earthen dam on the Teton River. The Teton Dam was one of several built during that time period using similar construction materials and design.

In the spring of 1976, the dam was complete and the reservoir behind it was filling for the first time. As the spring runoff brought the water down the river, the water level in the reservoir was rising four feet per day. The water level was nearly to capacity.

Only the relatively small emergency outlet works were in service at the time. The main outlet works and the spillway were not yet in service.

Officials observed water seeping through the dam on Thursday morning, two days earlier. Such seepage, however, was not considered unusual for an earthen dam and no extra precautions were taken.

At 7:30 Saturday morning, the seepage had become running, muddy water, suggesting there was a leak eroding the dam. Still not worried, no action was taken. By 9:30 in the morning, the dam featured a visible wet spot and water was spewing out and beginning to erode the face of the dam.

Crews with bulldozers were sent in to repair the leak at this point. Media began to arrive to follow the story. By 11:15 in the morning, officials announced the need to evacuate downstream communities. The bulldozers were sucked into the widening gap in the dam and their operators had to be rescued by coworkers using ropes as they scrambled on foot to escape the disaster.

At 11:55 AM, the dam collapsed, sending its contents down the canyon toward the communities of Wilford, Sugar City, Hibbard and Rexburg, the latter being by far the largest.

Teton Dam, June 5, 1976, by Eunice Olson.

That morning, 11 people were killed, most drowning, though at least one died as a result of the evacuation. Given that more than 10,000 people lived in those communities, many considered it a miracle that so few were killed.

Ultimately, 80 percent of the homes in the affected communities were damaged or destroyed. A lumber mill in the canyon provided the raging water with battering rams to aid in the destruction of property along the way.[1]

Rexburg is an old pioneer settlement with historical connections to other towns throughout the Mountain West. As a result, the surrounding communities, including Salt Lake City, organized a response, much as any community would rally in support after such a disaster.

Over the course of the summer, 500 to 1000 volunteers arrived daily on buses, typically bringing not only their own tools, but also their own food and food for the people they planned to help. By the end of the summer, nearly 100,000 volunteers had provided approximately one million hours of donated labor.[2]

When my father had the opportunity to go, he invited me, despite the fact that volunteers were expected to be at least twelve years old and I was merely eleven. I wasn't a big, strapping eleven-year-old who looked thirteen, either. I was short, rather pudgy (an adjective that has aptly described me virtually every day of my life) and was not likely to be able to do much apart from get in the way and queue up at meal time.

Our volunteer day remains one of the most vivid memories of my childhood—and one of the most foundational.

At 2:00 AM, one Saturday morning weeks after the disaster we gathered in Salt Lake City where I was living at the time and boarded buses headed north for Rexburg. We slept for most of the four-hour trip, arriving at sunup. We disembarked, downed donuts and some orange juice, grabbed our shovels and went where we were pointed.

We were assigned to work in a house that had earlier been condemned. It had been sitting for two months now with four feet of mud and water in the basement. In a rather ironic feature, it seemed to us, the home's chimney had been knocked out but the rest of the house was still standing. A

---

1   Wikipedia, "Teton Dam," (http://en.wikipedia.org/wiki/Teton_dam).

2   Eldon Linschoten, "Personal Impressions of the Photographer: Here's How I See It," *Ensign Magazine*, October 1976.

lone chimney standing as a tombstone where a house had once been seemed more fitting, somehow, than the reality we saw.

We worked in that house all day. I distinctly remember entering the house and smelling the mud, mold, mildew and muck throughout the home. The living room walls were marked where the water had stopped about halfway up.

Our first assignment was to remove the floorboards down to the subflooring so that new floorboards could be laid. I worked in the living room with the men. That work went quickly as the men worked ferociously to get the work done. A small bathroom on the main floor provided a dual challenge: a small workspace and more layers of flooring.

This became my special assignment and I recall working in that bathroom for hours on end. It was smelly, hard, frustrating work. I vaguely recall I ultimately had to summon help in order to remove all the damaged flooring.

Later, I worked to shovel the mud from what might have been appropriately called the mudroom, a small room off the kitchen through which people could enter the house, situated down a short staircase below the kitchen, but above the basement level. There was about a foot of mud in that room.

I still remember how heavy a single, small shovelful of mud seemed to be for this tired, eleven-year-old boy. I worked in that room with a team of others and do recall that we got it cleaned out, while a group of older men worked to empty the basement of four feet of mud.

We worked until the sun set, around 8:00 or 9:00 PM. We reboarded our buses and made the four-hour trip back to Salt Lake City, arriving after midnight.

I will never forget how I felt afterward. I'd never felt so good in my life. I'd certainly never been more tired.

Looking back, despite my exhaustion, I don't know if my presence had really made any difference at all. Though I have a vague recollection of someone who may have been the owner of the property where I worked coming by at one point during the day, I don't recall him or anyone else from Rexburg offering me a particular "thank you." Somehow, deep in my bones, I knew I'd done something good.

I made myself a promise then that I would never miss an opportunity to serve.

That promise, oft unfulfilled, has nonetheless provided a guide for me. When an opportunity to serve comes up, I still think of that promise and wonder how I might explain to my eleven-year-old self why I'm not living up to my promise.

Sometimes, however, I do serve. Sometimes I help. Not as much as I should. Probably not as much as you do. Certainly not as much as the people I'll tell you about later in this book. But sometimes, occasionally, once in a while, I live up to that old promise for just a moment and I remember how I felt back in 1976.

Introduction

You, the reader, have chosen to read this book because you have a desire to save the planet, to feed the hungry, to empower the downtrodden, to protect the vulnerable, to leave your mark on the world. For you, it isn't enough to accumulate a pension for 40 years and then spend 40 years slowly winding down. You have somewhere to go and something to do. Something that matters.

There are relatively few people in the world who have devoted their entire lives to solving world problems. Mother Teresa of Calcutta spent her life in service to the most impoverished people she could find. After becoming the richest person on Earth, Bill Gates and his wife Melinda, set up a foundation and have pledged the rest of their lives to serving others. There are many others, of course, but out of the entire world's population, they represent a tiny fraction of the human family.

The world is in desperate need of help from many people, not just a few. But the world also demands that most of us be engaged in productive activities that move a global economy forward so that more and more people have economic opportunities and can rise above the poverty level to participate in the miraculous world of technology and privilege that the vast majority of Americans and Europeans enjoy.

You can do it. You can leave more of a mark on the world than perhaps you ever suspected. It won't be easy, but it is certainly possible. Working patiently and strategically over time, you can leave an indelible mark for good in the world. This book will show you how you can do it, without quitting your job, leaving your spouse or abandoning your children—and without giving up all of the comforts you now enjoy.

Organizing Your Life

The actionable parts of this book will largely address personal and family financial planning, with a secondary emphasis on creating a sliver of time in your life for serving your chosen cause. Of course, time and money are closely related.

There are a variety of financial constraints in our lives that limit our ability to contribute to a cause as generously as we might like. Part of what this book will do is help you find those limits in your budget so that when you do contribute to a cause, you aren't giving away your retirement or what should be your child's college fund.

A fundamental premise of this book is that your money, your time and your heart should all be moving in the same direction. For some, perhaps most who read this book, the challenge is in moving time and money in the direction the heart has already gone. For others, I believe you'll find that your heart will follow your time and your money if you make the commitment to give only as a test; giving and serving with focus and dedication over time will bring joy and happiness that perhaps you didn't understand was possible.

Finding Your Cause

Scattered throughout the book, you'll find anecdotes of people who have served a cause or have been served by a cause. Most readers will connect on an emotional level to some of the stories, but not all. Don't feel like everyone who is passionate about a cause must be passionate about all causes; to the contrary, the point of this book is to encourage you to find a few things—maybe even one thing—about which you feel so passionate that it becomes yours.

By focusing your time and money on fewer things, you can have a much bigger impact. On average, people in the U.S. donate about 3.7% of their income each year to tax-deductible causes. Most of us spread that around, throwing "pizza money" at a dozen or two organizations and focusing a bit more on others.

Personally, I find it hard to say "no" to anyone who asks for money, so I continue to throw pizza money at just about any organization that asks. Those who were looking for something more in the range of "Rolex Watch money" generally don't call back.

By focusing your giving on fewer organizations you get the added benefit of easier record keeping. In recent years, I've found that well over 90% of my giving went to a total of three organizations (two dozen others got pizza money). If I had failed to keep good records of those pizza money donations, it would have had little effect on my tax refund.

If you have the courage I lack, to explain to others who ask, that you are now focusing your giving on your top priorities, you can get the benefit of even greater impact on your causes and even simpler record keeping.

How to Read This Book

This book will be presented along two parallel paths. Anecdotes related to causes I've found interesting will alternate with chapters that provide mostly financial advice to empower you to leave your mark on the world.

At the end of each story, you will find the contact information that will allow you to learn more about the cause associated with the story. Keep in mind that there are literally thousands of causes, not-for-profit organizations, charities, and opportunities to give. And the most valuable service you may give may not involve an organization at all.

A final note about style: as I approach this book, it feels deeply personal to me. I hope it will feel personal to you, too. As such, I'll use a somewhat more conversational style. You are the reader of this book. While there is a school of thought that suggests I should refer to you as the reader and to myself in the third person as the author, I hope you'll forgive my impertinence, but I've chosen to call you "you" and the author will generally be referred to as "me" or "I," as if we're having a conversation. My only regret is that this book is so one sided. I'd love to hear from you! I'm easy to find on-line (starting with my email address: devin@devinthorpe.com). I look forward to connecting with you on my blog, yourmarkontheworld.com, too.

Chapter 1

No Problem Too Big!

The scope of the world's problems lead many to shrug in frustration, thinking that the little they could do, would be too little to matter. For Matt and Allyson Smith and their six children, the opposite attitude led them to a remarkable around-the-world adventure in service. They seem to have left home in Idaho believing that no problem was too big for eight Smiths (and a few friends) working together.[3]

Smith Family, (left to right) Sam, Allyson, Brandon, Ashton, Charlotte, Matt (behind), Tyler (front) and Olivia. Photo by Tiffany Smith.

3   Most of the information for this story comes from a lengthy email exchange between Matt and Allyson and me, after meeting them in Cambodia in January 2012.

Their 15-week journey began in January 2012 with a visit to Cambodia (where I met them). There, they spent time working with the CICFO (easier than the mouthful "Cambodia and International Children Friend Organization") orphanage. Their first big project was to take almost 40 orphans across the country from Phnom Penh to Siem Reap for an excursion.

The Angkor ruins in Siem Reap are a UNESCO World Heritage site that, despite being just four hours away, none of the children had ever seen. The children stayed in a budget hotel funded by the Smiths that the children described as the nicest place they'd ever been. After returning to the orphanage, the Smiths built a chicken coop and then supplied chickens to provide a sustainable source of protein for the kids and for an income opportunity to help support the orphanage.

In Thailand, where the Smiths previously spent some time volunteering, they worked at two orphanages: The Home and Life and The Holland House. At the first, they helped the operators of the home to complete a restaurant and bakery that is now operated to make the orphanage more self-sustaining.

The Smiths' 15-year-old son Sam did his Eagle Scout Project at Home and Life, building a hydroponic, above ground vegetable garden designed to survive the torrential seasonal rains and flooding that annually wipe out the existing garden. He raised $2,500 to pay for the garden and then led construction of it himself.

Since leaving Thailand, Sam has received by email some photos of the kids harvesting and eating vegetables from the garden he helped them build. He notes, "It made me realize that with a little effort people can make a big difference in the lives of others."[4]

At the Holland House they just love and play with the kids, taking them on excursions, including a rare trip to the beach.

---

4   Sam Smith, Essay on the Trip, June 11, 2012.

Their daily routine would overwhelm most parents. Imagine the work of taking six kids on an around-the-world vacation. Taking six kids ages 3 to 15 on a 15-week service mission around the world and you begin to wonder if it is even possible. Each day starts with schoolwork so the kids don't fall behind their respective school programs back home. Then from noon to 9:00 pm they all work on the projects. Finally, they collapse into what might generously be described as their beds.

All six of their children, Sam, 15; Brandon, 13; Olivia, 10; Tyler, eight; Ashton, six; and Charlotte, who celebrated her fourth birthday during the trip, worked on every project. Just picture Charlotte helping another child to eat, dusting windowsills she can barely see or trying to shovel sand when she can barely lift the empty shovel.

That their teens and tweens would be willing to help is almost incredible, but Allyson's blog (http://carefreetimelessness.blogspot.com) is rife with photos of all six of the children actively engaged in all sorts of service—almost always with big smiles on their faces.

With the trip not quite halfway completed, Matt reported by email that Charlotte "just asked me where we live."

From Thailand, they went to India, where they visited Rising Star Outreach, a boarding school for children of parents with leprosy. They spent two weeks working in the school, learning to love the children, who would, without the school, be left to beg in order to eat and help support their suffering parents who often can't find work, even if they are physically able to do so.

After working with the kids, they next went to serve their sick parents. Ravaged by leprosy, the victims of the disease often lose their fingers and toes. All the Smiths helped to treat and comfort them, often cleaning and bandaging open wounds, sometimes infected with maggots.

Sam remembered one man in particular, Jayraj. Sam says, he "just wouldn't stop singing and dancing. We have the funniest video of him dancing and laughing. I was in awe. Here is this man who has no toes and barely any feet and is dancing and laughing and making everybody smile. He had the best attitude I've ever witnessed. As I thought about the things that I had complained about at home it made me feel like I was 2 feet tall as I watched him be happy amidst his trial. Whenever I feel bad for myself I always remember Jayraj, the happiest man in the world." [5]

One of the men they met there asked Sam, the Eagle Scout, about his career plans. When Sam said that he planned to be an entrepreneur, the old man looked Sam in the eye and said, "Always use your knowledge to bless the poor people of this earth."

There, they met a man who had borrowed less than $100 as part of the Rising Star micro-loan program and who now has 40 employees and runs a thriving business.

Another recipient of the micro-loans is a victim of leprosy who borrowed the money to buy the most rudimentary tools for giving a shave and a haircut and became a barber. Not only is he now self-sufficient, his wife—who had left him because he couldn't get work after his diagnosis—came back to him. The Smiths took time to clean and treat the open wounds on his leg that he carefully covers when he works to prevent hair from infecting the sores.

Early in their adventure, I asked about their biggest success so far; Matt replied, in part, "Watching our children love and work side by side with the children in the different countries."

He continued, "Our goal is to really help these children 'learn how to fish.' At each place we want to leave those we serve with something that will continue to help them. Also, as we build the projects, we want to teach the children skills such as woodwork, masonry, cement, tile laying, creativity and thinking."

Allyson said, considering her experiences and the fact that

---

5   Sam Smith, Essay on the Trip, June 11, 2012.

nearly one billion people in the world are hungry, "It causes reflection doesn't it? Do we really need a new handbag, pair of jeans, cell phone, designer shoes, or latest flat screen TV? Does there come a point where we put the jeans back on the shelf just to have some self-denial? To not give in to every want? Do we tell our children that we have enough clothes and we will make do with what we have already? Even if we can afford it, there is something to denying ourselves."

She added, "I am telling you right now that if you can get your teenagers to serve on a regular basis you will eliminate a majority of their—what's the right word for it—complaints, selfishness, laziness, and boredom. They will complain at first, but don't give up. Ignore it. They will thank you someday."[6]

In a final moment of reflection, Allyson recorded on her blog, "Throughout our service trip I have realized that we are experiencing just the tip of the iceberg. I feel like I am gobbling up appetizers again. The feelings we have felt and the joy that has been ours is leading us to the feast. We cannot go home now and not continue to give of ourselves. We know too much now. We have felt too much to go back and just be."[7]

Home and Life Orphanage Foundation
No.12/10 Pa-tae Moo6,
Thai-Muang sub district, Thai-Muang Distrct,
Phang Nga Province 82120. Thailand
Mr. Bhudit Maneejak (Root)
Mobile: +6681 951 3237
www.homelifethailand.com
homelifethailand@yahoo.com

---

6   Allyson Smith, "Micro Lending in India," *Carefree Timelessness*, May 5, 2012, (http://carefreetimelessness.blogspot.com/2012/05/micro-lending-in-india.html)
7   Allyson Smith, "Peace," *Carefree Timelessness*, April 23, 2012, (http://carefreetimelessness.blogspot.com/2012/04/peace.html).

Chapter 2

Finding Your Cause

You are an extraordinary person. You've proven that in a number of ways, I'm sure, but I can tell because you are still reading about how to organize your life and finances to be able to give more money away.

That's good karma.

I'm sure that you are the kind of person I'd like to meet, but more about that later.

If you have already chosen your cause and you know the organization to which you would like to devote your time and contribute your money, you can skip the first part of this chapter (or read it for sport and think about all the good people who may be joining you in your cause after you encourage them to read this book).

Causes are social. We like to engage in causes with people we love. There is nothing wrong with choosing a cause based on what your friends are doing, especially if that will increase your commitment and passion for the cause. Your friends can also help you determine whether or not the cause is legitimate.

If your friends aren't involved with something you would like to join, you may, of course, consider the causes mentioned in this book. Keep in mind, however, that these are a very small sample of the noble work being done in the world so don't limit your search. There are more causes and organizations mentioned on my blog at YourMarkOnTheWorld.com, too.

One of the best sources of information I've found on the Internet is GuideStar (www.guidestar.com), which provides a searchable on-line directory of causes. It is an effective, cheap and easy way to check on the basic legitimacy of a cause before you invest your life in it.

Ultimately, choosing a cause should be about finding your passion. If you can't get yourself truly excited about it today, it is unlikely that you'll get more excited about it tomorrow.

In writing this book, I hope to display an agnostic view toward causes. My goal is to help you do more for your cause, not to choose it for you.

You may wish to consider the following questions to help you choose a cause.

Which of the following categories most moves you to action?

Chances are, when you first started to think about choosing a cause, everything you considered was probably related to just one of the categories below:

- Animals (endangered species, animal cruelty, shelters, etc.)
- Arts and Culture (art, museums, cinema, theater, dance, symphony, etc.)
- Education (universities, public schools, private schools, special needs schools, schools for the impoverished, etc.)
- Environment (climate change, pollution, urban planning, etc.)
- Health (cancer, diabetes, cystic fibrosis, malaria, polio, HIV/AIDS, etc.)
- Human Rights (torture, political prisoners, women's rights, democracy, etc.)
- Orphans (foster care, big brothers/big sisters, special needs children, Chinese orphans, poverty-driven orphanages)
- Poverty (global hunger, local food banks, homelessness, income distribution, etc.)
- Religion (many consider their religion a cause; many religions provide humanitarian relief)

Of course, these categories overlap. Imagine, teaching impoverished orphans through a religious charity, where the kids are also treated for and vaccinated against disease and the kids are taught respect for the environment. That said, it is likely one or two of the categories above catch your attention.

Do you most want to help people in your community or those who are far away?

In the last decade or so, we have seen a growing effort to encourage people to buy locally grown food and to frequent locally owned businesses. The same logic that suggests you should eat at a locally-owned restaurant, would also suggest that you should focus on problems right in your community.

On the other hand, if you are interested especially in the plight of Chinese orphans, you won't likely find a lot of those unless you live in China. (China has a unique problem with orphans due to the "one-child policy" that has left nearly one million children abandoned in this enormous country.) The same principle holds for most endangered species; you may not find many in your local community.

Furthermore, you should enjoy your volunteering. For some, this means that the need you champion should be in an exotic location that you will enjoy visiting precisely because it is far away. If you have the means and the passion for travel, don't be ashamed that this enters into your thinking. Let it drive you. Let it stoke your passion.

How would you most like to spend the time you devote to the cause?

To really leave your mark on the world, you'll want to be thinking about getting involved with something where you will devote a lot of time over the balance of your life. If you are 35, you could be donating a few hundred hours to this cause for 50 years. That's a lot of time.

Give some serious thought to how you want to spend the time you devote to your cause. If you are a salesman, you may want more than anything to help take the fundraising for an organization to the next level. There are very few organizations that wouldn't want that sort of help.

On the other hand, if you just love children and want to devote your time and attention to actually caring for children—not talking about it or raising money for it, you'll want to focus on finding an organization where you can do that. If you can't afford to travel, you'll want to focus on local opportunities to help children.

So, whatever your interest, skill or passion, there is an opportunity out there for you to devote your time and energy to it. Think carefully about how you want to spend your time before you choose your cause.

A final note about what you like to do. Many people like to lead. The fact is, however, almost no organization will invite you to serve immediately in a leadership role. They want to see your passion and commitment manifested in time and money before giving you an opportunity to serve principally in a leadership role, say on the board of directors (either for the chapter or for the national organization). So, if you want to sit on the board of a local not for profit, prepare to spend some time doing whatever it is that the organization does or fundraising for it. Once you've demonstrated your commitment to the organization, you won't have to ask to serve on the board—they will invite you.

What sorts of causes have you found yourself contributing to in the past?

If you itemize your deductions, you had to make a list of your donations the last time you filed a tax return. You'll want to grab that list now to refresh your memory.

As you review the list, there are probably two kinds of causes to which you've given money in the past. First, those that have effective marketing campaigns that likely include getting someone you know to ask you to make a donation, whether or not you have any passion for the cause. Second, those for which you have a real passion that you sought out and helped in the past because you really want to make a difference.

Focus on the causes to which you have contributed that may be at the intersection of those two factors. A cause to which you've already given, that has a good fundraising campaign that includes one or more of your friends and that you are truly passionate about.

Ponder the Answers

After you consider the questions above and your answers to them, be sure to give yourself some time to ponder. If you are now in the process of defining your life's purpose, the activity that will give meaning to your existence, don't choose too quickly. Don't rush it.

You may want to try giving some time to a few different organizations to see how it feels. You'll at least want to narrow the candidates to a short list and begin researching them on the web to confirm their legitimacy, as well as finding out how you can help and what others think of them.

Be careful about considering reviews you read on-line. If you are considering getting involved, for instance, with a religious charity and you find a rant from a disaffected member about that cause, you can just ignore it. Look for feedback from the folks who believe and think like you. If you are interested in the environment, don't be discouraged by a rant from someone who thinks global warming is a left wing conspiracy. Choose your cause based on the feedback of those who share your passion—you're not alone in this.

So now we've circled back to where we began this discussion. Talk to your friends, including the person who encouraged you to read this book. Find out what she is passionate about. Chances are you'll find a place where you can work together to make a difference in the world and leave your mark on it!

Chapter 3

Rabbi with HEART

Nathan Pingor was completely out of control. He admits it. At seventeen, he was smoking cigarettes, sleeping around, street racing cars, flunking out of school and had completely abandoned his Jewish faith.[8]

The root of Nathan's troubles may lie in his parents' divorce at age two. Though he doesn't recall that being so difficult, when he and his mother moved from El Paso, where his father lived, to Houston, when he was seven, he began to feel his world unwind.

As a reform Jew, Nathan's mother, Melissa Fertel, felt strongly that she wanted to have her son educated in a Jewish day school where he would be taught values and history that would provide a "familial" connection, she felt was especially important following the divorce and the move to Houston. Ultimately, they chose a conservative Jewish day school that felt warm and welcoming.[9]

Although Nathan had a bar mitzvah at age thirteen, as is the custom, the family was not particularly religious; they didn't keep kosher or attend Shabbat services weekly.

By the tenth grade, Nathan was in real trouble. While he is very bright and even won the school-wide poetry contest that year, he failed every class. He was acting out, desperate to find a foundation for his life.

---

8   Phone interview with Nathan Pingor, July 3, 2012.
9   Phone interview with Melissa Fertel, July 3, 2012.

Finally, when he was 17, his mother sent him to Utah to participate in a short-term program for troubled teens at Outback Therapeutic Expeditions. Why Utah? Utah law allows parents to send their minor children to residential treatment centers where the teens are not allowed to leave; most other states allow the teens to walk out if they choose.

The program helped, but trouble continued so Melissa began looking for a boarding school in Utah where he could get the help he needed to finish high school and get his life back. While virtually every program she considered was non-denominational, she wanted to find a school where he would not be the only Jewish teen and where the program would be open to religious practice. She settled on Discovery Academy Boarding School in Provo, Utah when they told her about a Rabbi that regularly visited the school.

Nathan had been at the school just a few days, feeling angry and isolated, when one of the faculty told him that he had a visitor. Nathan says, "I had nothing else to do." He then met Rabbi Benny Zippel for the first time.

Within three weeks, Nathan had completely reconnected to his Jewish roots, he says he "picked up all the religion that I'd totally lost."

Before long, Nathan wrote a letter home asking his mother to send his siddur (prayer book), Hebrew dictionary and tefillin (artifacts used for a Jewish tradition that connects participants to God and to their heritage). Melissa was blown away by the request, and took it as a sign that her son was not only connecting with his roots, but finding a purpose in his future.

Rabbi Zippel has been visiting troubled teens in Utah residential treatment centers since the year the Italian-born Rabbi first came to the state in 1992. That December, nearly 20 years ago, the Rabbi received a call from the father of a teenager in a boarding school in Utah, asking that he go and visit him. He did; in fact, he began making weekly visits.

After a few weeks, he asked the teen if there were any other Jewish youth in the program; he responded that there were about a dozen. Rabbi Zippel began visiting them all. As he began to understand the national draw to Utah's residential treatment programs, he established his Project HEART (Hebrew Education for At Risk Teens), taking his message to schools across Utah—every week.

The service to the young people in these schools is deeply personal for Rabbi Zippel. He gets to know each one and connects not only with them, but with their families.

After every visit with Nathan, Melissa got a call from Rabbi Zippel, reassuring her that Nathan was doing well and that he was looking out for Nathan. After learning that Nathan had a special relationship with his grandfather in El Paso, Rabbi Zippel contacted a fellow rabbi there and asked him to visit Nathan's grandfather—which he did.

The father of a girl in one of Utah's schools, wrote, "I cannot put into words my sense of security knowing that Rabbi Zippel was in Utah looking out for my daughter's well being. His reports on his weekly visits gave us an independent report on our daughter's condition and mental state. He always could sense the emotional state of our daughter and would relay that to us in an honest and direct manner."

One of many success stories that Rabbi Zippel shared was of a young man who came to Utah for treatment. He visited with him weekly for a year. When they began their visits, the teen described himself as an atheist. When he graduated from high school, he moved to Israel, joined a yeshiva and became an observant Jew. When the young man married, he sent the Rabbi an invitation, not anticipating he could actually attend.

The date coincided miraculously with a trip that Rabbi Zippel made with Utah's Governor Jon Huntsman to Israel. When the Rabbi told him about the wedding, the Governor insisted that he break away from the group to attend the reception—which he did. That surprise reunion brought father, son and Rabbi all to tears as they celebrated more than a wedding that evening.[10]

Rabbi Zippel doesn't ask the youth or their families for money—nor does he charge the schools for his services, though they uniformly praise his work. He accepts donations to keep the program going.

Rabbi Zippel is an orthodox Rabbi from Chabad-Lubavitch, a movement within Hasidism that focuses on outreach and education for the broader Jewish community. Sue Fishkoff, a Reform Jewish author, notes that after spending a year researching Chabad-Lubavitch, she gained great respect for the organization.

She said, "I... have been touched by how Lubavitchers incorporate into their daily lives the Jewish values to which most of us give little more than lip service. They visit the sick. They comfort the grieving. They take care to avoid embarrassing others. Whenever I visit a Lubavitch home, I am urged to stay for dinner, if not for the entire weekend."[11]

Tami Harris, Clinical Chaplain at Heritage Schools in Provo, one of the schools that the Rabbi routinely visits, says that she routinely connects her Jewish students to the Rabbi, noting, "Even the kids who say they are atheists like him and participate. He just loves them and they feel that."

Tami notes, "For some of them it is life changing. He helps them feel God's love again. He reminds them who they are." She summed up her feelings, "It's wonderful to see them go from hopeless to hopeful."[12]

---

10 Personal interview with Rabbi Zippel in his office, July 2, 2012.
11 Sue Fishkoff, *The Rebbe's Army: Inside the World of Chabad-Lubavitch*, Schocken Books, 2003, page 6.
12 Phone interview with Tami Harris, July 3, 2012.

Rabbi Zippel, Nathan Pingor and his mother, Mellissa Fertel,
courtesy of Melisaa Fertel

Despite the Rabbi's regular visits, when Nathan turned 18, he left the Discovery Academy. He went straight to El Paso to visit his grandfather and stay with his father.

This was a difficult time for Nathan. He recalls one evening sitting on his grandfather's porch, when Rabbi Zippel called him. They spoke for 90 minutes. Afterward, Nathan decided to return to Houston to live with his mother, despite the fact that the Rabbi never took sides in Nathan's internal struggle between his parents.

Nathan says that Rabbi Zippel has had a tremendous impact on his life. "He's saved my life several times," he says, adding, "plus my relationships with others and with religion."

Living in the Bible Belt, his Christian friends will often use the phrase, "What would Jesus do?" as a decision-making guide. For Nathan, the question is, "What would Rabbi Zippel want me to do."

Nathan says, "He's absolutely, not only the best role model as far as religion goes, but the best role model in general. He's absolutely the best man I've ever known."

Chabad Lubavitch of Utah
1760 South 1100 East
Salt Lake City, UT 84105
(801) 467-7777
www.jewishutah.com
rabbi@jewishutah.com

Chapter 4

Making Time to Serve

Contributing money to a cause is really the easy part (of course, having some money to donate is not so easy and much of the rest of the book will focus on that problem) but giving time to your cause is much more difficult, especially for busy, career-oriented people.

The time challenge can be viewed through two primary lenses. The first is finding a way to help; the second is freeing up the time to do it.

Let's start with finding ways to get involved in your cause. There are as many ways to get involved as there are causes. For most causes, broadly defined, there are a large number of specific organizations that are tackling the problem in different ways.

For instance, if fighting poverty is your cause there are countless organizations, from local, community based organizations that operate shelters and homeless outreach programs to national organizations that do so in many communities under a variety of banners, like Volunteers of America and the Salvation Army, to international organizations that work to alleviate hunger and poverty, like Unicef and the Red Cross.

You may wish to get involved with a local organization or the local chapter of a larger organization, in either case, your involvement likely starts with a visit to a website to learn about upcoming events and activities.

If they have no other operations locally, most chapters of large organizations at least have a grassroots fundraising effort in most major cities so chances are you're not far from someone who is doing something for a cause you're already passionate about.

Fundraising activities seem simple and painless from the standpoint of a donor, but most take hundreds of hours to organize and execute. Many fundraisers involve dinners, long distance running, or cycling races. Any of these sorts of events requires the help of volunteers; I've never heard of an organization turning down an offer to help.

As you get involved this year in helping to plan and organize a fundraising event, you may find yourself pulled into leading a committee responsible for organizing a future event. If you do that well, and especially if you are donating money to the same organization, you'll be getting the attention of the organization's local leadership. At the same time, you'll start to feel real ownership of the events, you'll have real relationships with other volunteers (and paid staff, if there are any) and your passion for the cause will also increase.

The result is that within a few years of such service, you'll find yourself likely serving in a leadership capacity that will give you an opportunity to really make a difference in the organization. It won't be long before you'll see how you are making a real contribution to the organization, to the community and even to the world.

And all of this can be done with only five to ten hours per month—much less time than would be required for a part-time job.

So let's consider how we find the time or make the time for service.

First, we have to make service a priority. You need to decide how service to your cause(s) fits into your personal hierarchy of values. The central thesis of this book is that you should be able to make this work around your current job and without leaving your spouse or abandoning your children. Not only do you need to begin to think about how your volunteer time fits with your current obligations, but you'll also want to talk to your employer and your family about your goals and get their feedback.

Many employers make time formally or informally for their employees to do significant volunteer work in the community, some even allow for that while employees are on the clock. This is part of their effort to be good corporate citizens as well.

In the event that your employer isn't supportive, knowing that is important before you get yourself over committed. Finding opportunities to serve around your work schedule should not be difficult; the need is limitless and the chances to serve are plentiful. It is important for you and your boss to understand each other when it comes to what amount of service is realistic given your current work commitments.

You'll want to have the same sort of conversation with any family members, especially a spouse, who may be impacted by your involvement. Ultimately, you'll want your family engaged with you and your enthusiasm should eventually draw them naturally into the cause with you. In the meantime, if your volunteering will take you away from family a few hours each week, it is wise to make sure everyone understands your goals and your time commitments so they can support you and make your contributions less of a sacrifice.

Now, you personally do not watch too much television. We know this because you are reading a book, which by definition precludes watching television right now; and, because you are cause-oriented it is unlikely that you watch as much or more than the average amount of television.

According to a Nielson ratings survey conducted in 2009, the average American watches 151 hours of television per month. So, allowing that you watch much less than the average, you may still be watching 50 hours per month. Finding 5 to 10 hours of time pulled from television should not be too hard.[13]

Our other leisure activities are vital to our mental health; we all need time to decompress, but looking at the time we spend on Facebook and other social media sites just for fun can also provide a source of time for our service contribution.

Please note that I am not suggesting that you give up television or Facebook in order to volunteer. Personally, I can't imagine giving up either one of those things! But, I would suggest that as we seek to find time to volunteer five to ten hours per month, one of the sources of time may be our casual leisure time spent in front of a screen.

Altogether, time contributed by your employer, supported by your family and reclaimed from television and/or Facebook should allow you the time you want to do the good you want. You can do this. You can leave a mark on the world!

---

13   "Television Viewing at All-time High," *Los Angeles Times*, February 24, 2009. (http://articles.latimes.com/2009/feb/24/business/fi-tvwatching24)

Chapter 5

"I am a witness of God's love for these babies"

For Amanda, her life can most easily be divided into two parts: preparing to run the Starfish Foster Home in Xi'an China and then running it. She feels her life prior to launching the home in 2005 was divinely led, including some bitter trials, to prepare her for saving some of the most vulnerable people in China—special needs orphans.

Amanda's Mormon faith is central to who she is and why she serves the way she does. She was not born into the faith; rather, she joined the Church of Jesus Christ of Latter-day Saints (the formal name of the Mormon, or LDS Church) when she was a young woman living in Rhodesia.

Later, she served a proselytizing mission for the Church, which she was very reluctant to do. She described it as both painful and difficult. Still, she counts that time as one of three keys to her preparation for her work in Xi'an.

After her mission, she heard one of the faith's Apostles, Neal A. Maxwell, speak at an event in South Africa, where she was raised and was living at the time. He described the role of Jesus Christ not only as taking upon Himself the sins of the world, but also its suffering. This insight began to map a course for Amanda's life that would point her toward a place where eventually she would have the opportunity to facilitate the relief of suffering as an expression of her faith.

Amanda visited the United States in 1988 to attend a friend's wedding. She ended up staying for 18 months and decided she wanted to attend school there. She returned home to complete the application process for Brigham Young University, but was rejected because her grades weren't quite where they needed to be.

She applied to Utah Valley Community College (now Utah Valley University) and was admitted. She spent a few semesters there but was then deported over an administrative error related to her visa.

This window in her education proved to be important in her life, because she went to Taiwan to teach English for a year while she worked to obtain a new student visa. Thus began her connection to China. While there, she applied again for admission to BYU and was rejected again.

With help from friends, she returned to the community college and continued to work on improving her grades. This time, she was successful. Her third application to BYU was approved and she earned a degree in Family Science, a discipline that she describes as a "cross between social work and psychology."

Upon graduation in 1996, she returned to Taiwan to teach English. Shortly after arriving, her sister back in South Africa divorced and was at risk of losing her children. Amanda committed formally to provide financial help from her meager teaching salary to help her sister so she could keep the children. This locked Amanda into a job she'd thought would be temporary. After six years her sister was able to find employment and Amanda was free to pursue her own career.

Expecting to quickly obtain a permanent work permit in Taiwan, she quit her job and began looking for a new one. She quickly learned, however, that she would not be granted a permanent work permit and so needed to find a position elsewhere. On a whim, she checked for positions in China and found one in Xi'an and in less than an hour had a position. She packed up and left.

Once in Xi'an, she immediately began looking to volunteer in an orphanage. The first people she approached about volunteering told her there was no orphanage in Xi'an. She later found a woman, Laura Shang, who worked at the orphanage doing international adoptions that helped arrange for her to volunteer there.

After several months of volunteering, Amanda became discouraged, feeling like her help was tormenting the children rather than blessing them. She'd visit the orphanage and scoop up a child and love him or her for an hour and then leave, perhaps never to see that child again. She felt like she was teasing the children by showing them such love and kindness as they had never experienced before was possible, only to leave them in a world without it.

She expressed her frustration to Laura, who suggested that she start working as a foster parent. Amanda couldn't believe she'd be allowed to do it, but with Laura's help, she was approved to foster an unlimited number of babies for ten years. This actually scared Amanda so much that she asked for the contract to be rewritten with an annual renewal (a decision she now laughingly says she regrets).

She began with just a handful of children that she kept in her apartment, mostly with volunteer help. As she added children, she added volunteers and then some paid nannies. She also added more apartments as she expanded. Finally, in 2010, she found a more permanent location that comfortably serves more than 50 babies—when she has them.

There are days in the foster home when she thinks, "If I can get through another day it will be a miracle." She adds, the challenges of her LDS mission prepared her for those times.

She sees miracles in so many things that have happened, allowing her to bless and serve more children. As the end of 2011 approached, Amanda received a call from the President of her Board, Patrick McLaughlin, reminding her that the organization had only two months of cash. What, he asked, was she planning to do? She says she responded simply that Heavenly Father would provide.

And He did, she says. Within a few days, the organization received unanticipated donations of $170,000, providing enough cash for a year!

"I am a witness of God's love for these babies."

Three children at the Starfish Foster Home in Xi'an, China.
Photo by Devin Thorpe.

It wasn't long after that miracle, however, that Amanda's whole world changed. After not feeling quite herself for some time, Amanda finally sought medical attention and learned the devastating news that she had stage four uterine cancer.[14]

After receiving a round of chemotherapy in China, friends found a hospital in Tennessee that would treat Amanda for free. After arriving there early in the spring of 2012, she received additional treatments, regained her strength and be-

---

14 This story is a product of interviews with Amanda de Lang, Cindy Klaja-McLaughlin, Julie Monson, Patrick Belnap and others who have worked with Amanda. The interviews were conducted in March and April of 2012. On March 23, I spent the day at the Starfish Foster Home, meeting the staff and learning more about the operation (Amanda was already in Tennessee for treatment at that time).

gan looking forward to the possibility of returning to China to care for her children. Summer, however, brought other news. The cancer had stopped responding to treatment.

Faced with the choice of continuing painful and ineffective treatments or entering hospice, she chose the latter. On July 14, 2012, surrounded by friends, she peacefully passed away.

During her final week in the hospital, one of her friends heard her say, "168 babies, nearly 250 surgeries, and 81 adoptions - that pretty much sums up my life."[15]

A Love Story

In 2007, shortly after Patrick McLaughlin sold his media business, he and his wife Cindy Klaja-McLaughlin arranged to volunteer some time at Starfish Foster Home in Xi'an, China.

While they were there, they met and fell in love with their daughter whom they now call Xi'Xi, pronounced "she-she," (her given name is Norma Xi'an).

Given both China's one-child policy and that many hundreds of millions of people in China live in poverty, it is understandable that babies born with medical problems are frequently abandoned by their parents. China does not publish reliable statistics about orphans, but it is believed that there are between 500,000 and one million orphans there. Most, now, are special needs children.[16]

The stigma of having a special needs baby, combined with the cost of treating one is really only half the problem. China's infamous pollution is apparently to blame for a rapid increase in the number of birth defects.

The children at Starfish are all special needs children, most of whom were not thriving in the public welfare orphanages that the Starfish Foster Home serves.

---

15   Eve Boger, email, July 14, 2012.
16   http://chinaadoptiontalk.blogspot.com/2010/07/amy-eldridge-of-lwb-speaks.html

Starfish partners with the public welfare orphanages in both Xi'an and Yuling, to the north of Xi'an, to rescue babies that might otherwise be left to die. Anecdotal reports of rooms where babies are left to die are ubiquitous on the web; statistics don't add up, so it is hard to determine how many may be dying. What does seem clear is that the public welfare orphanages have traditionally tolerated a high mortality rate and have done relatively little to save kids who, for whatever reason, don't do well in the public orphanages.

In July of 2007, Starfish received word from the Yuling orphanage that there were two babies with spina bifida who were candidates for their program. Amanda De Lang, Founder and Executive Director of Starfish, sent two staff members to get the babies. Upon arrival, they found there was a third.

Xi'Xi was among the three babies brought to the home that day. Xi'Xi was born with hydrocephalus and encephalocele, or cranium bifidum, leaving an opening in the skull with an associated protrusion or sac.

Amanda remembers that when Xi'Xi arrived, she was in constant pain. Most spina bifida patients are not in acute pain, but poor Xi'Xi made a near unbroken sound like a cat's meow, her weak and feeble effort to endlessly cry out for relief.

Xi'Xi was struggling to survive when Patrick and Cindy arrived in Xi'an in early September 2007. They immediately fell in love with her and asked what they could do to help her. Amanda responded that they could pay for the surgery she needed in Shanghai.

"Done, what else can we do?" was the answer. Xi'Xi got the surgery she needed—and with it relief from pain—and after 14 months of progress, Patrick and Cindy adopted her.

She received additional surgeries after coming to the United States. She suffered from strabismus (crossed eyes) and from frequent ear infections; both were treated surgically in 2009, shortly after arriving in the U.S. In 2011 she also had cranioplasty.

Now about five years old and living in Manhattan, Xi'Xi is happy and vivacious. "She has a marvelous personality and is physically beautiful," says Cindy, adding, "Pat and I think these two gifts from God will far and away make up for any deficits resulting from her development delays." She charms everyone she meets.

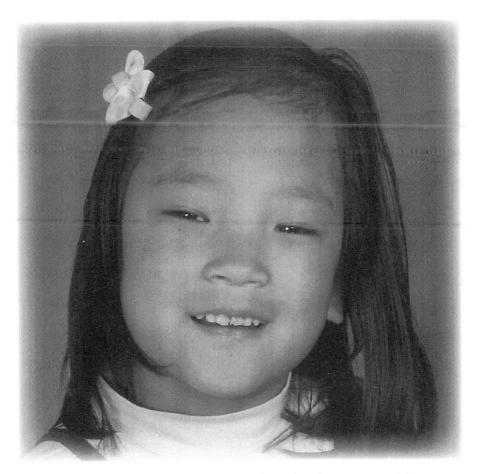

Xi'Xi, Norma Xi'an, courtesy of Cindy Klaja-McLaughlin.

Virtually all of the children that go to Starfish have the same experience. They are loved and cared for, treated and prepared for adoption. Nearly 100 children have been treated and adopted through the Starfish Foster Home.

Along the way, a bond of friendship developed between Amanda and Patrick and Cindy that has lead them to help Amanda form a board of directors to shoulder some of the fundraising load so she can help more kids like Xi'Xi. Starfish would not exist without Amanda's founding drive, passion and energy, but Patrick and Cindy have helped expand the impact Starfish can have and are working to help it make a transition away from near total reliance on Amanda.

Patrick and Cindy returned to their busy lives in New York City after their visit to Xi'an, but Cindy describes the change in their lives ever since as an "ongoing out-of-body experience."

Cindy is the vice president of innovation for a consulting firm called Maddock Douglas and also runs her own marketing strategy firm, Watt an Idea!!! Inc. Patrick is now the director of business development for a company called web. com. Despite their busy schedules, they make time not only for Xi'Xi, but for helping to grow the Starfish Foster Home in Xi'an.

Cindy and Patrick epitomize the thesis for Your Mark On The World; you can make a big difference in the world without leaving it all behind. You can leave your mark on the world along the way.

And what a mark they will leave.[17]

Starfish Foster Home
Attn: Naomi Kerwin
ChangLeGong Department for Old
Mid FengJing Road
XiaoLiuZhai Village
WeiYang District
Xian 710018
ShaanXi Province
CHINA

---

17 This story was developed from a series of interviews and email exchanges with Cindy Klaja-McLaughlin and Amanda de Lang in March and April of 2012.

Attn: Patrick McLaughlin
Board Chair
6 West 122nd Street
New York, New York
10027
USA
(917) 494-7691
www.thestarfishfosterhome.org
paddymac0130@gmail.com

Chapter 6

Budget To Empower
Your Mark On The World

There is power in a budget. Don't think of a budget as crimping your style or limiting your options. Think of a budget as a key part of your plan to leave a mark on the world you can really be proud of.

By simply eliminating waste from your spending through carefully budgeting, you can put yourself into a position to donate ten percent or more of your income to your cause every year without giving up much—if any—of the things you enjoy most today!

While some people may discover in the process of budgeting that fixed obligations and consumer debt, may already consume too much of their income to give 10% or even half that amount to a cause today, careful budgeting over just a few years can empower generous giving and at the same time allow you to solidify your financial future.

Making a mark on the world, in part, by giving generously to your cause, is not something you need to do instead of building a safe and secure financial future for your family. You can do both at the same time. Budgeting is a key part of how you can do that.

Let's consider for a moment that if you are 35 years old as you read this and you hope to donate 10% of your income for the rest of your career through age 65 to your cause of choice, then we are talking about a lot of money! We're talking about making a very large contribution to an organization, except that it will be the sum of lots of little contributions.

Let's assume you earn $100,000 per year. We'll use that number because the math is easy. (You can extend the idea to your particular circumstance easily by adjusting the following conclusion by the ratio of your income to $100,000 simply by dividing your income by $100,000. If you make $50,000 per year, then $50,000 over

$100,000 = 1/2 or 50%. Multiply the result below by 0.5 to see how much you can contribute in your career. If you make $175,000 per year—congratulations, by the way—you do the same math and ultimately multiply the result below by 1.75.)

Ten percent of $100,000 per year represents $10,000. That is a very large gift for virtually any charitable organization. You will quickly find yourself on the "President's List" or some other list of notable donors to your cause because you are making a mark immediately.

Let's consider, however, that the value to the organization you plan to give that much to every year means your commitment has a present value of many multiples of that amount, but easily would be comparable to more than a $150,000 one-time donation today.

Furthermore, if you were giving to an endowment where your donation is invested to help support future costs, as with a University, you'd see your annual contributions over the course of 30 years with modest compound returns (most endowments seek to spend less than all of the return from the endowment so that it grows each year purely from investments to support ever-more activity in the future) would grow to over $500,000 during your career.

That's quite a mark.

Now, let's get to work on that budget!

Preparing a budget

In order to prepare a good budget, it helps to know where you are already spending your money. Unless you've been keeping track already, you'll likely be surprised. I know, believe me, I'm always stunned by finding out how much I've spent on eating out!

In order to figure out where you spend your money, you need to find a way to identify all of the spending. If you don't have a system in place, you'll want to start with all of your bank statements and credit card statements for a couple of months. Our goal will be to put together one complete month—then we'll talk about some annual expenses and other periodic expenses that may not be hitting your budget every single month. Because bank and credit card statements rarely begin and end on the first and last of the month, you'll likely need two months for each institution to nail down expenses for one month.

Now that you have a stack of statements, you should be able to go through and identify all of your routine spending. You can see on your bank statement all the checks you wrote (if any) and all of the cash you took from the ATM.

You'll want to create a ledger. If you like computers, you may want to use a spreadsheet, but you can do this on paper fairly easily. We'll be doing some addition and subtraction, but no higher math.

As you identify each expense on your ledger, write the category of spending along the left hand side of the paper. So, when you look at your power bill, write something like "Utilities" along the left hand side and then write just the amount of the power bill to the right of the word "Utilities." Do this for every expense you can identify for a month.

Then, add up all of the expenses you found for each category. Under "Utilities" you probably wrote down several items, one amount for the power and another for the water, sewer, gas, and maybe the cable bill. Add up those individual amounts to determine your total monthly spending for "Utilities"—and for every other category.

Then add up the total of all the categories. Let's hope that the total is less than the sum of your income—which we'll want to check now.

Look at your paychecks for the month. You can simplify your life if you ignore all the deductions and just budget for the things that don't come out of your paycheck to begin with. (That said, some nerds like me, like to add all of the payroll deductions to the monthly spending budget and work from the gross payroll amount.)

Now compare your income to your expenses. Chances are, things look pretty good—because so far we're ignoring expenses that don't hit every month.

You'll want to budget savings for quarterly, semi-annual and annual expenses that didn't turn up during your chosen month. Check older statements for things like property taxes, car insurance, life insurance, summer vacations, Christmas spending and the like.

If you are like most of us, that good feeling you had a few minutes ago is starting to fade. Never fear! You can do this.

You can match your income to your expenses, add savings and even take some additional money out for your cause and make it work. How do I know? Because someone on your street is almost certainly living on 10 or 20 percent less than you make. It may seem impossible for you right now, but think about it, if you took a 10% cut in pay, the world wouldn't end; you would just have to cut back. You'd prioritize, you'd make do and you'd be fine.

Celebrate the opportunity you are embracing now to take control of your life, to take control of your money to empower you to make your mark on the world.

Once you have matched your income to your basic expenses, you're ready for the real work. We'll work throughout this book to come up with a budget for saving for future events so that you can be sure you're saving enough. We'll talk about the tax advantages of saving and of giving to your cause and you'll be amazed at what you can do—if not this month—very soon.

Power Comes from Discipline

Once you've created a budget, the power and influence you want to create in the world are close enough to touch. In order to make your mark on the world a reality, you have to find ways to actually use the budget.

Think of following your budget a bit like following a diet or a work-out regimen. The results you want don't come from writing down the plan to go to the gym, the results come from going to the gym, getting on the equipment and working out until you're drenched in sweat— over and over again.

Getting control of your finances requires the same sort of discipline. Look for tools and processes to help you.

Generally, there are just a few problem areas in a budget. You won't need a reminder not to make your mortgage payment twice, or a tickler to remind you not to pay the dentist again, but you may need to find a mechanism to track the number of visits to Starbucks, how much you spend on Christmas presents this month or how much you spend on eating out.

For things you generally use cash for, you can use this simple trick: figure out how much you've allowed yourself in your budget for the week, pull out that much cash from the ATM on Monday morning and don't go back to the ATM again until next Monday—don't cheat and use your ATM card at Starbucks when you run out of cash!

For things you generally use a credit card for, you'll need to find a way to check your spending against your budget. Most credit card companies now make your spending history available on-line. Without any expensive or time-consuming software, you can just check your credit card statements on-line once or twice a week to compare your actual spending to your budget.

The long-term results and your power to really make a difference in the world will come down to finding the self discipline to live within your budget on a day to day basis. So when you find yourself arguing with your conscience about how badly you need a Starbucks stop, re-member the starving children in Africa, or the endangered polar bears whose habitat is melting, or whatever cause you choose, but remember your purpose, your vision, your goals for making the world a better place one tiny sacrifice at a time.

Measure Your Progress

For most of us, the best part of budgeting is counting the money, seeing the progress and then doing something powerful with it.

Every month, quarter or at least annually, you'll want to sit down and carefully assess your budget performance, looking both at how you've done against your budget and at how much money you've accumulated.

Before we're done with this book, you'll have set savings goals for retirement, your children's college education and perhaps you'll have created a sabbatical fund as well. You'll also have a target for building cash reserves and all of this will roll into your plan.

You will find the results can be dramatic after just one year, especially if you have little saved now. If you go from saving none of your income—which is typical in America—to saving 10 or 20 percent of your income, you'll be amazed at how much is accumulating.

You'll also be able to look back and see what you've contributed to your cause—even if your donations the first year are modest—you'll have tracked what you donated and the sum of a year's contributions will be meaningful.

Make a formal budget review something you do with your spouse, so that you measure your progress together. Celebrate the milestones, large and small, together. Don't point fingers, assign blame or insult one another over budget variances. Nothing in the budget is more important than your marriage, so keep perspective. If you've aligned yourselves on your goals and made plans together, chances are good that you're both doing your best.

A budget variance may be a sign of a legitimate error in the budget, not the spending. Many things you'll have little control over, like car insurance premiums, property taxes and the like.

Even within the discretionary categories in your budget like clothes and restaurant dining, if you've budgeted too little, you may just make yourselves miserable.

By talking openly and honestly about your goals for making a difference in the world, for financial security and your day-to-day needs and wants, you can build a budget that will allow you to live happily and do great things.

Every family is different. Some are happy to drive a clunker or live in a home well beneath their ability to afford a home, while others would gladly give up virtually all discretionary spending just to have a home in the right neighborhood or keep a new car in the driveway.

That said, if your budget is under pressure, the solution may not be to cut back further on your daily spending but to look at the big budget busters: your home(s) and anything that you have to take to the gas station (cars, motorcycles, RVs, ATVs, snowmobiles, boats, jet skis, etc.).

We all think of our home as our biggest expense, or at least our biggest investment. It is huge and vitally important. We'll talk more about homes and how to finance them later, but the first piece of advice I'd give you is to stay put if you already own your home.

In contrast, your cars and the other things you may own that require you to gas them up are the source of that proverbial great sucking sound you hear. The easiest way to fix up your budget is to sell the toys and use the cash to pay off consumer debt. We'll talk more about that up ahead.

Remember, you can right size your spending to allow you to both save for the future and make meaningful contributions to your cause today. Take courage, you're on your way!

Budgeting Tools

There are all kinds of tools to help you with your budgeting. In this day and age, most now take advantage of the Internet to automate many of the tracking tasks that we used to have to do manually. I bring this up at the end of this chapter, however, to make a point. The budget is the important thing, not the tool.

If you start your budgeting exercise with choosing a tool, you risk burning up your available time and energy for budgeting with a frustrating trial and error of buying and trying to learn software rather than figuring out how much your discretionary spending should be each month.

In the long run, however, most people will find that having a software tool will make tracking your finances easier and more productive than using a simple spreadsheet or the old paper and pencil method.

Once you've built a budget and begin working to live with it in order to create the world you want for yourself and your family, you'll likely want to buy a software program to help you.

A quick search of Amazon.com provided a list of 72 different options. Over the years, I've used Quicken and found it to be an extremely powerful tool. I love computers, technology, numbers, and money so this stuff really floats my boat. So don't judge by my experience. Chances are you're reading this book because you don't like numbers, you're worried about money and not master of it, and you probably don't like math!

More recently, I've been trying a new, free, on-line service at Mint. com. It is owned and operated by the Quicken folks and doesn't require you to do anything but set up secure access to all of your bank accounts and credit cards. It will (attempt to) do the rest for you. It will not only categorize your spending, it will (attempt to) build a budget for you.

Of course, it really can't do all of that. You can correct the errors and fill in the gaps fairly easily and with a little bit of time you'll find that it is not too hard to use and can be quite helpful.

Mint.com doesn't charge you a fee because it will regularly send you updates and alerts about your financial situation and suggest ways you may be able to save money by using a product or service offered by one of the Mint.com sponsors. Personally, I have a high tolerance for such news and don't feel unduly tempted to follow up on every suggestion for earning a fraction more interest here or saving a penny on every brokerage commission there. Let's be clear, I am not a Mint.com sponsor. They don't pay me to include this reference in the book.

It really is beyond the scope of this book to do a thorough analysis of the available options for personal financial planning software or for me to teach you how to use it, but there are lots of books out there that will help you with such things if you want that sort of help.

Chapter 7

Raising a Pig in the Apartment

Before the night Pol Pot's men came and began killing the people in her small Cambodian village apparently at random, Botevy's father—a colonel in the King's army—warned her and the family to hide their valuables and take cover. When the gunshots rang out, ten-year-old Botevy led her family, except her father, running for the pond to hide in the bamboo.[18]

Botevy's mother, with her youngest son just six months old in her arms, came last, calling to Botevy, "Avy! Where are you?" Botevy coaxed her toward the seeming shelter of the bamboo. More shots rang out, followed by the cry of her mother, "Help, Help me! I've been shot!"

By now, about ten people from the village were hiding in the bamboo. One of the men volunteered to crawl out to rescue her mother as Botevy's grandfather hushed the children. Botevy, in desperation, quieted the youngest by covering their mouths with her hand.

Once her mother arrived in the bamboo sanctuary they determined that her wound was relatively minor; she'd been shot through the palm of her hand and the same bullet had torn through her brother's tiny calf. Both would clearly survive.

---

18 This story is drawn from notes that Botevy and her friends have made in preparation for what may someday become a book about this remarkable woman, and from my visit with her in Phnom Penh.

In the morning, her father helped to get the wounded to the hospital. Then he warned the villagers that the fighting to come would be much worse than the night before. Following their father's advice, they fled to the central part of the province of Svay Rieng.

There, life took on a semblance of normalcy. Botevy attended school and even competed on the basketball team. But normalcy was limited; people lived in constant fear as the Khmer Rouge tightened its grip on the province. Shelling made everyday life dangerous; families slept together, terrorized, in bunkers.

As the Khmer Rouge victory became apparent, Botevy's family, led by her father, moved to Phnom Penh. Once the Khmer Rouge declared victory, however, they announced that everyone must leave the city for their "home land" for three days. Everyone took their valuables but otherwise packed light, expecting—or at least hoping—to return within a few days.

Botevy's family had a small car; they loaded it full of their belongings. The family walked beside it. They couldn't even get the car out of the city due to the throngs of people attempting to leave. Ultimately, something between chaos and anarchy developed. The Khmer Rouge were killing people indiscriminately, fires broke out and panic erupted.

Botevy ran through the streets trying to find her father, stepping over and then on the dead bodies. At one point she stepped on a pregnant woman she thought was sleeping; she stopped long enough to determine that the woman was not sleeping but dead and then kept running over and among the corpses that the soldiers had left in long lines.

Ultimately, she found her father. They traveled forward, constantly on the lookout for her mother from whom they had become separated, finally abandoning the car and taking an antique ox cart to use to carry their belongings. After a week, they were reunited as a family.

Botevy believes the family only survived the Khmer

Rouge checkpoints as they slowly made their way through to the countryside because her mother spoke up at each one, cleverly lying about her father, describing him not as a Colonel in the now defeated army but as a teacher. Her father never corrected her in front of the soldiers, but he insisted that this was unnecessary, as clearly they would want the benefit of his skills and leadership in their organization. History, of course, would prove the wisdom of his wife's deception.

Their trip from Phnom Penh back to Svay Rieng is 122 kilometers and it took them 30 days to complete the trip on foot.

At the border of the Svay Rieng province, the Khmer Rouge soldiers, perhaps recognizing her father as a former soldier, invited him to answer a few questions. As the hours passed, the anxious family waited. Finally, the soldiers came out to tell the family to move along, to return to their home in Svay Rieng and that their father would soon follow. Botevy begged to see her father and for some water, but her cries went unacknowledged as the soldier left them.

The family had no choice but to follow his instructions. They covered the remaining 30 kilometers in two days, among the endless parade of people uprooted from the cities, returning to rural communities where they may or may not have had surviving family members waiting to greet them. Botevy's family slowly made their way to her paternal grandfather's home, where they stayed only a few days.

While there, they were trained in the ways of the new regime. Everyone was to be equal—equally poor peasants. Anyone desiring otherwise as evidenced by talking, or resisting in any way, was clearly an enemy of the new regime and would be summarily shot.

As she settled in to the new routine Botevy and her family constantly worried about her father. One day, while working in the fields she saw him in a line of people, walking. She tried to follow him but was chased off by the soldiers marching the prisoners.

As the prisoners were marching by her father's home, he was able to persuade the guards to let him stop and talk to his father. Botevy's grandfather sent for her and she begged permission from her work group leader and was able to go talk to her father for the last time.

On another occasion, Botevy and her mother were assigned to harvest rice in a location far from their normal assignment. One of the workers there told them that her father was being held in a home that could be seen off in the distance. Pretending to work, the two women slowly made their way to the makeshift prison and asked the guards if they could see Botevy's father. Not surprisingly, the answer was negative. After a time, however, Botevy's father appeared in the yard at some distance from them. He pretended to exercise and appeared to ignore them, but it was clear that someone inside had recognized the two women and told him to go outside to see them. The women called to him and cried. It was the last time they ever saw him.

It would be many months before he died in prison, as Botevey would later learn, as a result of a combination of torture and malnutrition.

During this period of time, Botevy was assigned to work and sleep with a group of girls that included a girl she'd known from Svay Rieng called Ouk Vanneth; they'd played basketball against one another. When they first reconnected in the camp, Vanneth asked how Botevy was doing; she said she was well, but added, "I miss my mom and dad." Botevy was crying now; Vanneth whispered to her, "Don't be sad. Make your face look happy; they look at us." So they smiled through their tearful reunion. That tenuous connection provided the beginning for what was to become one of the most important relationships in her life.

During the years she spent harvesting rice, there was never enough food to eat. The "peasant farmers" like Botevy who worked in the fields were not allowed to keep or eat any of the rice they harvested. Instead, their erstwhile hosts provided inadequate rations. Many people did not survive. Botevy's mother was clever and had managed to bring from Phnom Penh some medicine that she was able to use to barter for food to keep her family alive during the worst times.

At age 17, Botevy was married. Under Pol Pot, the Khmer Rouge, or Angka as they called themselves, arranged marriages. As you would expect, most such marriages failed. Now, 34 years later, Botevy remains married to her husband, the father of their three girls.

Botevy became pregnant within three months. It was a difficult time, near the end of Pol Pot's rule. Food was exceptionally scarce. Botevy was nonetheless able to give birth to her first daughter, Ya Ya. Today, Ya Ya works as a hairdresser in her own shop in Phnom Penh, not far from where Botevy lives.

The Vietnamese army liberated Cambodia from Pol Pot. Botevy's family was able to avoid the fighting that took place during those battles, though many of the peasants took up arms during that conflict to fight against the Khmer Rouge.

Botevy settled in Phnom Penh with her husband and began work as a teacher in a primary school. Two years after being married, she saw Vanneth one day but only in passing—they didn't even have a chance to talk as they both rushed to their respective jobs.

When Botevy's third daughter was born in 1985—Botevy was just 24—she quit her job at the primary school and began working an evening shift at a hotel and doing sewing at home during the day. They didn't even have enough food to eat. Seven-year-old YaYa had to take on adult responsibilities, like shopping and preparing meals so Botevy could work.

Life was a constant struggle for resources. There never seemed to be enough food to eat. In desperation, at one point, Botevy and her family tried raising two pigs in their third floor apartment.

In 2002, Botevy determined that learning English could help her find better employment. As she looked for resources in the community to learn English, someone told her about a church that was teaching English. She found the church, which was in fact offering classes in English.

Botevy began attending church and one Sunday discovered her old friend Vanneth seated on the row in front of her, old friends joyfully reunited. Botevy's family ultimately joined the church.

In 2005, Botevy, Vanneth and another friend from church, Tom Sophany, decided to join together to organize an orphanage. They found twenty children and began caring for them on some land that Vanneth's ex-husband owned. They registered the "Children Rehabilitation Organization" with the Ministry of the Interior. Initially, they funded the operation from their own meager resources, but later attracted some support from the west.

The three did not make a great team and after a year the outside funding dried up and they were forced to close the orphanage. They filed the paperwork with the Ministry to close the orphanage, but the children begged them not to send them back to the villages they'd come from. (Most children in Cambodian orphanages have parents who are too poor to care for them, but often they maintain some contact with them).

Botevy and Vanneth together decided to do what they could for the children. They could scarcely feed the children initially, but once again began to develop relationships that allowed them to access some outside funding. They registered a new organization, Cambodian and International Children Friend Organization (CICFO).

Today, there are many orphanages in Cambodia registered with the Ministry of the Exterior and operated by foreigners devotedly serving people in a country that is really just beginning to recover from the terrors of its modern history.

According to Botevy, however, there is only one orphan-age that is registered with the Ministry of the Interior and operated by local people: Botevy and Vanneth's Cambodian and International Children Friend Organization (CICFO).

Botevy, pink shirt at the rear of the group, and her kids.
Photo by Devin Thorpe.

Over the years, they've helped 50 children and currently serve 31 in the orphanage today. They do all they can to provide for their own needs, growing mushrooms, raising chickens, and making bracelets. They recently acquired a lathe to allow them to make souvenirs that can be sold to help fund their operations.

What they earn, however, doesn't come close to covering the food bill each month. The staff are all volunteers; no one is paid. The kids are all in school and receive English lessons as well. They also have learned music and dancing (when I visited they performed traditional Khmer dances beautifully).

When I asked Botevy how she had been able to find a place in her heart to devote her life to caring for other people's children after all she'd been through, she seemed to struggle with the question, not because she didn't understand the English, but because, as she ultimately explained, she does this "because" of all she's been through, not in spite of it. She knows how challenging life can be for poor children in Cambodia and she's doing something about it.

Cambodian and International Children Friend Organization (CICFO)
Phnom Penh, Cambodia
www.theglobaloutreach.org
keobotevy@yahoo.com

Chapter 8

Aligning Your Income

There are few sorrows, however poignant, in which a good income is of no avail. ~Logan Pearsall Smith, "Life and Human Nature," Afterthoughts, 1931[19]

Your Goals and Values

As you begin to think about your financial planning in the context of your desire to leave your mark on the world, you'll find it helpful to begin with an analysis of your goals and values.

The premise of this book is that you want to leave to your posterity or to the world a good gift, a gift that will almost certainly require money but that will be to you and those who receive it something greater than money. You will find that if you contribute time and money to a cause they work together synergistically, allowing you to receive more happiness from sharing than you'll feel you've given.

As you consider your income and income requirements, you'll want to consider the cost of your goals and objectives relative to your income and the time you have left between now and retirement. For instance, if you'd like to endow a scholarship at your alma mater with a $1 million gift within the next ten years, you likely need a different level of income than if you have thirty years to achieve less financially costly goals.

It is vitally important to the success of your plan that you be realistic about the income objectives you identify today. While I would never want to suggest to anyone, least of all you, that you can't achieve whatever goal you set for yourself, my objective is to help you achieve the sheer joy of successfully giving what you hope and plan to give. If you set a goal to endow a scholarship with $1 million and later give only $750,000, I would hate for you to feel that you have in any way failed.

---

19   www.quotegarden.com

Additionally, I find that pairing your money and your time gives more meaning to your giving. The import of this observation is that you, and perhaps the organization(s) you choose to support, will find it more meaningful to give less of your money and more of your time.

As you consider what is truly important to you, I imagine there are some people you love who may represent a piece in the puzzle we're assembling. You may want to make specific allowance for the needs of your spouse, your children and even your parents or other loved ones. In what ways do you want to be a resource to them? Time? Money? Temporary housing? Long-term housing? Please let me encourage you not to think of these considerations as obligations that need to be calculated into your budget, rather think of the people you love and the opportunities you want to create to serve them.

Then, as you think about your career and the income you need to accomplish your objectives, factor in the time you want to spend with your loved ones and in service to your cause. This means that you may be choosing not to earn the maximum conceivable amount that your training, skills and chosen career path allow, but instead you will seek to bring balance and harmony to your life, making time for family and service to your cause.

You'll want to be truly thoughtful about your goals and honest with yourself before you make plans. For some, it is important to be able to see the faces of the people they help. Others prefer to stand back from the action. Perhaps the demands of your career and your drive for achievement don't allow you to devote much time to your cause, but they may allow you to devote a great deal of money to it.

Whatever your circumstance, be honest and realistic about your objectives because they'll be with you for a long time. Your greatest opportunity to shape the future will likely come from committing now to a cause that you can support for many years. The goals you set now should be crafted to motivate and inspire you not just ten days from now but for years to come.

Second Incomes

There are two sorts of secondary incomes that you should consider carefully before you chase them: moonlighting and having both spouses work out of the home.

Let's consider the latter first, as I suspect some will be very concerned about what I may say.

Having both spouses work out of the home may be the happiness-maximizing thing to do in your family for a variety of reasons. First and foremost, if you both want to work, then you should. End of story.

Now, let's consider a hypothetical situation where one spouse, let's say you, works as an accountant for a Big 4 firm and, having been there for six years; you can now see you are on track to make partner. You are now approaching a six-figure income with your thirtieth birthday still ahead and two young children at home.

Now, let's assume your husband earns less than half of what you earn. In the United States, the tax code is rather punishing to your husband's income. Taxed with your income, he'll pay tax at a much higher effective rate than you (presuming we count your income first). Your first dollars earned are not taxed at all. The next dollars are taxed at a low rate and the next are taxed at a higher rate. All of his income will be taxed at the higher rate.

To add insult to injury, you're both paying social security and medicare taxes on every dollar of your income (although, once you make partner, your income will certainly reach a point during the year where you won't have to pay social security taxes—just in time, perhaps, to pay for Christmas shopping).

So, your husband's income is really less productive than yours, given the tax structure. To be clear, the rules aren't gender based, of course, so if your husband is the prosperous accountant and your income is less than half of his, the same logic applies—the spouse with the lower income (the one you could consider living without) is effectively taxed at a higher rate.

Now, in addition to the tax issues, consider those expenses that are incurred only because you are both working. Two such items jump off the page. The first you'll think of immediately. If you're paying for childcare because you both work and your husband could stay at home with them, then we should deduct the childcare expenses from his income. Now, if you also have a second car that you could do without if he weren't working that would likely save you even more money each month than the childcare.

We'll talk more about cars later —a lot more—but let me just say that a typical car is costing the family more than $500 per month, and a nice car or truck could top $1,000. If he is driving a relatively new, $30,000 truck that gets crummy gas mileage, costs a fortune to insure, is depreciating several hundred dollars every month, and for which you've borrowed money at 12% interest just to buy it, it may well be that between taxes, the daycare and the car, your hubby really isn't contributing much to the family budget. He could stay home, watch the kids, sell the truck and contribute just as much.

So, now, ask yourself again if you both really want to work. Of course, you and he may both say "absolutely!" And, of course, you could likely sell the big truck and buy a little econobox clunker for what the truck costs every month and start putting most of that $1,000 the truck is costing right back into your pockets.

Now, I admit that I've thrown a lot of numbers around without a complete and thorough analysis of your situation. As a general rule of thumb, most people who are earning more than $40,000 per year are really contributing to the household budget—but if that income is the second income (by second, I mean smaller), it doesn't likely contribute as much as you think it does.

If you'd like to evaluate your personal situation more carefully, please talk to your accountant (unless like the woman in our example, you are one). You may also wish to use the online spreadsheet I've prepared for you at yourmarkontheworld.com/tables.

Let me say a word or two about moonlighting. Having been an employer in the white-collar world I am familiar with, I've always been concerned about the commitment of people who are moonlighting. They were not on the fast track for advancement and in fact were often on the list of those who might be let go in the event of a corporate downsizing.

Those who do shift work and can manage the sleep deprivation and the other headaches that may come from working two jobs, more power to you. We see too little of that old American tradition of sacrifice today. There are some work-at-home positions that may work for a stay-at-home spouse. For instance, there are many people in the world who earn a full-time income from network marketing, working largely from home. Without jumping into a lengthy debate about the pros and cons of network marketing, let me add that most people who try networking are not successful—it is really hard work. Those who are most successful seem to be the ones who most hate their current situation and who have had good incomes in the past.

More and more contact centers or what we used to refer to as "call center" type jobs are moving home. Jetblue was a pioneer in this area and many companies have started moving their customer service staff home. This may appeal to some who can avoid virtually all of the expenses associated with a job that requires you to dress well, eat out for lunch, and drive a car across town to work. Few, however, will allow you to "work" and watch young children at the same time. Generally, these opportunities don't pay as much as the best jobs in the market, but many people still do them simply for the work-at-home convenience and other fringe benefits (i.e,. health insurance, flight discounts, etc.).

However you choose to earn your living as a family, take a look at your long-term goals and objectives then work to harmonize your life, making your employment a part of a balanced and fulfilling effort to leave a legacy.

Earning v. Spending – the tax effect

As you think about your income goals and plan your future, it is easy to plan for more money to cover expenses; it is harder to actually earn it. This dichotomy may be the biggest reason that saving is so difficult.

One of the key reasons that earning money is difficult is that our marginal income is taxed at the very highest rate that may apply to us. Like with the discussion of the two income family above where your husband happened to earn considerably less than you, but his effective tax rate was higher than yours, the last dollars you earn are taxed at the highest rate—usually well above your effective or average tax rate.

The highest tax bracket in 2012 is 35%, meaning that the most the IRS will take from your paycheck is 35%. Remember, however, that they don't start taking that much until you're earning a rather nice income and then they don't apply the rate to all of your income (earning more money will never mean you keep less than you would when you made less income—though in some cases your employer may withhold taxes for you in a way that causes your net paycheck to go down when you get a raise, don't worry, you'll get the difference back when you file your tax return).

The point of this discussion is this: the next dollar you make will be worth less to you than the first dollar you made and it is likely to be worth less than 65 cents when you take into account federal taxes, social security taxes, Medicare taxes, and state and local income taxes.

The uptake here is that if you want to earn an extra $500 to buy an iPad3, you'll come up short if you quit working after you earn the extra $500 because of incremental taxes. If you took the last $500 you earn, it would only net you about $325. In order to save $500 for the iPad, you'll need to earn almost $800. That makes the iPad look a lot more expensive, doesn't it? (The exact ratio will depend on your specific tax bracket, but the principle—if not these exact numbers—applies to everyone who earns an income in the U.S.)

So as you consider your income and spending plans, for most of us in the middle class, we will ultimately find it easier to save money by controlling spending than by finding ways to earn a little extra money.

Chapter 9
Life Beyond Limits

With a four-month-old baby and without having celebrated her 30th birthday, everyone was surprised when Laura Pexton was diagnosed with breast cancer. It was difficult even for her to find another person who was going through this at her age; most caregivers could not think of anyone else who had been diagnosed with breast cancer so young.

It was emotionally trying for Laura, but she did chemotherapy and radiation and put her life back together and moved on. The cancer did not.

In November 2004, Less than three years after her original diagnosis, she had been experiencing chronic back pain and no one seemed to be able to figure out what was causing it. Finally, she learned she had a fractured L5 vertebrae resulting from cancer in her bones. Her entire skeleton, it was learned, was infected by the c-monster.

The doctors cemented three vertebrae in her back and blasted her with huge doses of radiation. The doctors also wanted to put her back on chemo. There was, however, no prospect that chemo would provide a cure at this stage, so she declined. About this time, however, a new drug was introduced, Herceptin, that treats certain kinds of breast cancer. She started on the drug eight years ago.

After the second diagnosis, Laura describes herself as "wallowing in self-pity," feeling terribly sorry for herself for being such a young victim of a disease that would not only take her life, but that would rob her of so much joy in the time she had left.

Laura credits God for lifting her out of the abyss. At Stanford University, near her home, she got involved in a study using Healing Touch, which she described as "a hands on healing modality promoting relaxation and energetic balancing of the body's energy system." During these sessions she began to experience real peace as she learned first to recognize then to shut off the painful thoughts swirling incessantly in her mind. "Don't believe everything you think," she admonishes.

Drawing on her Christian faith, Laura says the New Testament phrase, "Peace I leave with you, my peace I give unto you…" came repeatedly to her mind bringing an enduring sense of calm and hope. "Let not your heart be troubled, neither let it be afraid."

Over time she felt guided from one book to another, from one teacher to another, each in turn, lifting her spirits and miraculously strengthening her physically. She continued with the cancer treatments every three weeks but otherwise was living an essentially "normal" life, as the cancer was considered "stable."

In 2006 she received the shocking news that the cancer had spread to her brain. After an appointment to plan for Cyberknife treatment, Laura decided to attend a class called Art and Imagery that happened to be starting right then at the cancer center.

A nurse coached the participants to "go to a favorite, comforting spot." As Laura struggled to envision such a place, she found her paradise was hidden on a desolate island where she otherwise didn't want to be. The vision of her little paradise veiled on the otherwise barren island became a metaphor for her life, which seemed desolate and barren as a result of the cancer, giving her hope that she would yet find joy in her future.

She underwent Cyberknife radiation to treat the brain tumor and it never returned.

After a time she recognized a desire that seemed ridiculous for one who was suffering from a terminal illness, but she began to dream of serving on another medical mission. A trained nurse, Laura had done three medical missions to Russia and Kenya with Operation Smile before her baby was born and her life had been unalterably changed by cancer. It seemed absurd to be thinking about doing that again in her condition.

In 2007, notwithstanding how absurd it might seem, Laura nervously paid to join a medical mission organized to repair cleft lips and palates in children disfigured by these defects in Urumqi, China. Although exhausted as the team traveled to the other side of the world and performed nearly 200 surgeries in less than two weeks, Laura enjoyed every minute of it.

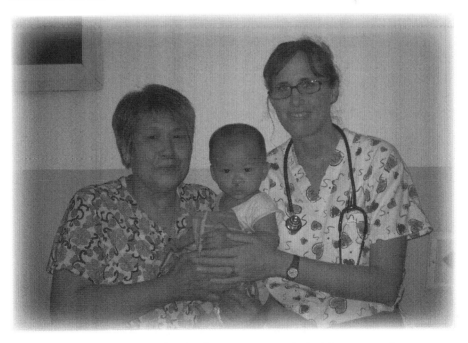

Laura Pexton, right, and a patient with his foster mother in China in 2007. Photo courtesy of Laura Pexton.

Of the experience, she said, "To watch these children gaze wonderingly into a mirror and see their new smiles was priceless. Parents frequently wept with joy and gratitude."

Since the 2007 trip to China, Laura has been on seven more medical missions to destinations all around the world—sometimes surrounded by filth, stench and squalor, lacking basic medical supplies, running water, toilets, and electricity. She's worked with both Operation Smile and with IVUmed, an organization training local surgeons and their teams to do surgeries on children with problems of the kidneys, bladder or genitalia.

Cancer has not stopped tormenting Laura, but she doesn't let it stop her. Less than 24 hours after returning from a mission to Ethiopia (where she's served twice) in 2011, she broke her pelvis. Since then, she's recovered and has been on more missions.

Laura notes that her life is full of irony. It is, she says, "interesting how polar opposite my life is. I'm healthy and I'm sick. I'm a patient and a healer." It may be that no one is more amazed by this than Laura, herself. She has hiked the Great Wall in China and parasailed in Vietnam. She was rattled by an earthquake in Peru and the team endured a typhoon in Vietnam, where she has been on two missions. She has also been to Senegal and India. She often doesn't tell the people she travels with about her diagnosis and they would never guess from looking at her.

She is "surprised," she says, by the growing attention to her story. Local magazines and a news reporter have done articles about her and she is regularly asked to speak to groups about her travel, her service and her condition.

She says, "It has been a profoundly, humbling experience. A power higher than me has worked through me. If it were up to me, I would have been sniveling and groveling and I'd be dead. Instead, it has been a miracle. I choose to follow my intuition: stop focusing on your pain and start focusing on what you could do!"

While in China she met a sweet foster mom who brought in a one-year-old girl to have her cleft lip repaired. This child also had a congenital heart defect and had been abandoned as an infant, with her umbilical cord still attached. The heart had previously been repaired and now that the lip was fixed the foster mom told Laura through an interpreter, "Now she have good heart. She have nice smile. I hope she find good home." This woman taught Laura that one person can make a difference—a lesson Laura takes to heart.

Her frequent missions around the globe have taught her something else, she says, "It's possible to live beyond limits"; adding, "Listen to that voice buried inside and you won't believe where your soul will take you."

Putting it into clear perspective, she says, "When you're serving others your problems just sort of melt. It is just amazing to me. It is so humbling to see where I was and where I am."

Laura also credits her husband for providing financial and emotional stability to keep her going.

Now ten years after her original diagnosis, she is making long-term plans again. With no plans to suspend her travel, she is starting a PhD program so she can gain access to public health data that she hopes to use to really make a difference in global health. Cancer interests her, but she is really driven by the desire to make a difference in health care for the billions of people on the planet who don't have access to the sort of care she herself received.

Laura embodies the spirit of leaving your mark on the world.

Operation Smile
www.operationsmile.org
Operation Smile
6435 Tidewater Drive
Norfolk, VA 23509 U.S.A
Phone: (888)-677-6453

IVUMed
ivumed.org
3269 S. Main Street, Suite 230
Salt Lake City, Utah 84115
Phone: 801-524-0201
info@ivumed.org

Chapter 10

Funding Your Mark On The World

As you approach this notion of really making a difference in the world by giving time and money to your cause, you will quickly arrive at a moment of truth. At some point, you've got to begin writing some big checks to support your cause.

Don't panic. You can do this.

First of all, I know you. You've already been giving money to a variety of causes and some of the money you'll give to your primary cause can and should come from the money you've been scattering around.

Among the 40 million people who itemized deductions and identified charitable contributions in 2002, the average percentage of adjusted gross income deducted was 3.7%. Furthermore, more than 27% of these 40 million households reported donating more than 5% of their income and 12.4% reported donating more than 10% of their income.[20]

Given that you are reading this book, I'm willing to bet you've already been giving more than the average. As you work through your plans, you may find that you can easily begin giving 10% to your cause immediately. If not, I suspect you can start with 5% now and work up as you choose in the future.

A few of you may realize after thoughtful consideration that you've been giving away some money you should have been saving for retirement or for other purposes. You may need to cut back slightly, at least to start, but as you pay down debts and increase your savings you should find your monthly budget improving, allowing you to return to your more generous ways quickly—but doing it more prudently.

The balance of this book is designed to help you identify meaningful ways to reduce your spending so that you can refocus that cash flow on your cause, while at the same time ensuring you have enough squir-

---

20 Joulfaian, 2005

reled away for your children's education and your retirement. We'll even help you create a savings plan for a sabbatical service year (or half year, or three months).

You may be such a kind person—and there are a few of you out there—who wonder why save for yourself for the future when there are starving babies in Africa? You can even make the case that humans may cause the extinction of so many more species on the planet within our lifetimes that it seems to make living for the future nearly pointless. Lives and life hang in the balance, right? The time to make a difference is now, right?

There is more than enough tragedy and suffering to go around. That's precisely why you're reading this book, to find out how to do more to solve those problems. Let's remember, however, that there is one thing for sure that will not help feed the hungry or end global warming and that is your becoming a cause. If you systematically give away all of your income and assets and find yourself living from paycheck to paycheck, you are suddenly just one paycheck away from becoming a problem that needs to be solved. Let's make sure that you are always in a position of being able to help and not putting yourself at risk of becoming the need.

Of course, all of us need help from time to time. Who among us can truly claim to be self-made? Everyone has someone. There is nothing wrong with having needed help. Don't be ashamed. Be grateful to those who helped you. But don't let your generosity put you at risk in the future. Use the principles of this book to allow you to be both generous and secure so that you can give today and tomorrow.

The U.S. Tax Code

Thank heaven for the U.S. Tax Code. Wait! Don't throw this book across the room just yet—you might break something you can't replace—you'll see my point in a moment.

Even the most liberal among us, those who believe in the role of government to make the world a better place, wish that the government could do it a bit more efficiently. Then there are those among us at the other end of the spectrum who believe the government has no role but for the national defense are particularly chapped by the whole (unconstitutional, they argue) idea of a federal income tax. Just to test the hypothesis about how much we dislike actually paying our taxes, check your return for last year. Did you include a tip? No? You didn't leave an extra 10 or 15% for the feds? OK. Let's agree we don't like paying taxes.

So the great thing about the tax code is that when we itemize our deductions using form 1040, we can reduce our tax burden. For most of us, it matters quite a bit to our total tax bill.

While most people in America have a fairly low effective tax rate, their marginal tax rate is generally at least 28% with a state tax kicker.

Let me take just a moment to explain what I'm talking about here. Your effective tax rate is the tax you pay compared as a percentage to your adjusted gross income. So, if you earn $100,000 and pay $15,000 in federal tax, your effective tax rate is 15%. (There are separate tables for single people and married people and for kids or others who are dependent upon someone else. A variety of other things impact these rates, too.)

For 2012, a married couple filing jointly pays just 10% in tax on the first $17,000 of taxable income. A good chunk of your income is tax-free income because the couple is entitled to income exemptions for themselves and for any children they have. That is one of the key differences between your adjusted gross income and your taxable income.

The next $52,000 earned is taxed at 15%. Income above that in our example is all taxed at 25%. For those who earn considerably more, there are 28%, 33% and 35% tax brackets. Those top rates were higher until President George W. Bush led a tax cut that was scheduled initially to expire after 2010; Congress has extended those cuts through 2012 to help spur the economy, but they could rise in the future. (IRS.gov)

After settling up with the I.R.S. you'll also need to settle up with your state, where the same principles may apply. If we assume that your state imposes a marginal tax of five percent, then that would bring your total tax rate to about 33%. (I say about, because generally the state taxes are deductible on your federal return, effectively reducing the tax rate a bit.)

So the bottom line is this, the federal and state governments are likely subsidizing your contributions quite a bit, by about 1/3, in fact. So if you donate 10% of your income, the net impact on your cash flow for the year will be just 6 to 7% of your income. If, as we've already established, you've been more generous than the average American, already been giving five percent of your income to charity, then bumping up to 10% of your income will only cost you about 3.6% of your income. You are closer than you think to becoming a 10% giver!

Now, there is a key to making this true. You must be able to deduct more than the "standard deduction" on your return or all of what I've said about the federal government subsidizing your gifts to charity doesn't apply. You must be eligible to itemize your deductions by virtue of having eligible deductions in excess of the standard deduction.

If you earn more than $100,000 per year and give 10% of your income to charity, you will be able to donate part of the money above the value of the standard deduction. For those with lower incomes, the standard deduction will be larger than your gift, meaning that unless you have other items to deduct, you really won't be getting a tax benefit for your contribution.

The easiest way to increase your tax deduction is to buy a home and borrow the money to do it. About sixty percent of Americans already do, so if you are in that majority, you are all set. Your mortgage deduction is likely similar in scale to the standard deduction, meaning that most or even all of the charitable contributions you make will be effectively deductible and will thus entitle you to the itemized tax deduction discussed above.

Many financial planners will suggest that you should never pay off your home, that you should leave your mortgage to your kids, along with the home, because the after tax cost of the money is so low. They are not crazy and it makes perfect mathematical sense. That said, I diverge from the consensus on this matter. If you can pay off your mortgage, do it. It guarantees you a place to live and will give you peace of mind that is invaluable. Furthermore, while the math supports the consensus plan, the long-term impact is small according to my analysis. If you are fortunate enough to own a home without a mortgage, I would not suggest getting a mortgage to increase your tax deduction, I would celebrate the fact that you don't have a mortgage (or rent to pay) and so have an even greater financial capacity to give—with or without a big tax break.

A Few Final Thoughts

First, every situation is different. I've left out about 14 volumes of tax code and simplified several things, so don't think of this as tax advice. You need to get that from someone who actually knows your situation. I've provided a broad overview to help you see that you can do this. You really can give more and have more impact than you ever thought possible.

Second, all of this stuff can be confusing and frustrating. You don't need to understand all of it to understand this: charitable contributions often can be deducted from your taxable income, reducing the taxes you pay. It is more often true if you make a mortgage payment rather than paying rent, so it is another reason to buy a home.

Finally, keep reading because we'll talk more about ways to reduce your spending so you can get these great tax benefits and leave your mark on the world!

Chapter 11
Maasai Mary

Mary knew what was coming as she approached her 13th birthday. And she would have none of it. In a place where babies aren't recognized as people until they are three "moons" old, because infant mortality is so high, Mary was lucky to have arrived at the ripe old age of 12.[21]

Mary didn't stick around to be mutilated and married off like so many of her elder peers had been. Instead, Mary ran away to create for herself a different life, one where she could make a real difference to her people. Though her father had passed away, her uncle chased after her, hoping to bring her home so she could become a traditional Maasai woman. Mary traveled for two moons to find a place where she could be safe.

Female circumcision is still widely, though not universally practiced by the Maasai people in Kenya. It is against the law, but still viewed as essential, even by some girls who may be viewed as unmarriageable if they aren't circumcised. Most commonly, an outside practitioner using knives and blades fashioned by a blacksmith performs a clitorectomy. The procedure not only leaves women scarred, but it also may adversely affect their ability to urinate.[22]

---

21 The bulk of the content for this story came from an interview with Shosho on April 7, 2012 and from follow up email correspondence with her thereafter. Additional information came from the Africa is Life Changing web site, http://africaislifechanging.org.

22 Wikipedia, "Maasai."

Life for a Maasai woman is not easy. Being seminomadic, their homes are not permanent dwellings. Built by the women on a frame of sticks; mud, cow dung and human urine are used to complete the circular or star shaped homes, called Inkajijik.

Shosho, Vicki L. Stone, the American founder, of Africa is Life Changing, found Mary in school on the Maasai Mara, living with a Christian religious leader. She was one of only three eighth grade girls in a school with perhaps 100 boys. Shosho challenged the three girls to do well on their final exams, promising that the girl who had the highest score would receive a scholarship to attend the new Africa is Life Changing boarding school for girls, St. Catherine's School. Having interviewed the three, Shosho anticipated that Mary would be the one who would make the effort to have the highest score.

Indeed, Mary earned the highest score on her exam and earned that scholarship spot in the new school. There, she excelled in her subjects and demonstrated her leadership ability. Whenever a teacher asked, "Who would like to..." Shosho says Mary's hand was up before the teacher could finish the sentence.

Mary graduated from the high school and went on to college. She has now completed nearly two years at the university and is planning to become a teacher. Shosho says Mary's desire is to "influence her people in many different disciplines."

Mary's success has also allowed her to reconnect with her family. Having accomplished so much, they are proud of her and welcome her home when she visits.

Africa is Life Changing (AILC) is an organization that is working to empower women and children in Kenya, battling the AIDS epidemic there through education, medical treatment and community action. Each year, AILC organizes an expedition to Kenya where volunteers help to do special projects related to the ongoing mission of the organization. These include construction projects at the school, HIV-AIDS prevention and treatment education, classroom teaching at the school, and training local co-ops of women life skills to help them provide for and raise healthy children.

Shosho, Mary and Sana (Gloria Terry). Courtesy of Shosho.

Mary is seen in the photo with Shosho and Sana (Gloria Terry), Africa is Life Changing Founders. Of Mary, Shosho says, "She is a very powerful young woman and one we are keeping our eyes on."

Now, Mary will leave her mark on the world.

Africa is Life Changing, Inc.
1192 East Draper Parkway, Suite 255
Draper, UT 84020
USA
Tel: (801) 471-6336
africaislifechanging.org
info@africaislifechanging.org

Chapter 12

Your Cars Can Help Your Cause

Your cars really can't help. Don't let anyone or anything convince you that buying a new car will help your cause (unless General Motors is your cause)

Cars are the giant budget suckers we park in the driveway that prevent us from reaching our financial goals. The only way your cars can help your financial plan is when you choose to make decisions that will save you thousands and thousands of dollars over time that can go toward your cause.

If you are like me, there is not much in the world that is more fun than buying a new car. Everywhere you drive, again, if you're like me, you see every car as an advertisement for that car. Some ads are not very compelling ("drive me, and you, too can be stuck on the side of the freeway during rush hour instead of being on time to a job you don't like anyway"). Others are very seductive ("drive me and everyone will think you are smart, powerful and good looking.") It is hard for me to tune that all out. Do you know what I mean?

So I want you to be very careful. Nothing I say in this chapter is intended to make you go buy a new car today. I say that because if I were reading this chapter, I would try to find the message that said, "Devin, you need to go buy a new car today to save the planet and rescue orphans."

If you find that message in this chapter, I apologize. I've miscommunicated.

The number one best thing most people can do to help their financial situation with respect to their cars is to simply keep driving them. Boring. I know.

Most cars built in the last twenty years or so were designed to go 100,000 miles without needing major repairs. Most people don't drive their cars that long and some like to buy a new car every year or two.

Recognizing that the general rule is that you should keep driving the cars you have, let's consider the possibility that you could or should sell one or more of your cars.

As you began working on your budget, did you discover that you are under some pressure because of too much debt or not enough income? Are you struggling to find a few dollars to put into savings or to give to your cause? If your budget is really under pressure then the possibility of selling a car should be a consideration.

Give your transportation situation a serious evaluation by asking a few simple questions. What is the ratio of licensed drivers to cars in your home? (Over the years, I have known a few people who actually have more cars than people to drive them!) Is public transit an option? Before you say no, ask yourself the question this way: do any of my neighbors use public transportation to get to and from work? If they can, maybe you can.

It will probably surprise you, but a fairly basic car is likely costing you $500 or $600 per month. More people own cars that cost them more than $1,000 per month than realize they do! Let's say you bought a Dodge Durango (a mid-size sport utility vehicle) last year for $35,695 with no down payment in a state where license and registration rules require you to pay a total of 7% (including sales tax) for a total of $38,194 the initial payment on a five-year loan would be $737 per month, well short of $1,000 you say? Wait a moment.

For the first several years you own the car, it will depreciate much faster than your loan payments reduce the balance of the car loan—but we can ignore that for now.

In addition to the car payments, you have to buy insurance. Insurance will likely be in the range of $100 per month on that vehicle, varying widely depending on your age and driving record.

The car won't go anywhere unless you add some gas. A tank a week at $50 per tank brings you to about $200 per month for gas and we're already over $1000 before we get to maintenance. Admittedly, with a brand new car there won't be much maintenance needed for a while, but just about the time your car payments have brought the loan balance into line with the value of the car, you'll have to start replacing brakes, tires and other parts of the car that wear out.

Bottom line, even without driving a top of the line automobile (even a top of the line Durango would cost another $10,000 with options) you can see what a tremendous financial obligation a car represents.

If you are in a position to sell a car and not replace it, there is no financial reason I can think of not to do that today. Right now. Go sell your car if you don't need it and then come back and finish reading this book. I'll wait.

OK, at this point, I presume that you either can't sell a car without replacing it or you've already done that and you're back to read the rest of the book. (Wink, wink.)

May I confess something? I didn't choose the Dodge Durango at random. The Dodge Durango was, for a time, my dream car. Smaller than a Chevy Suburban and a bit less expensive, it featured a third row of seats so I could haul lots of people around (a very important feature in a car for a guy with one wife and one son). So, I went out and bought one brand new. I got it with the big, giant engine and the fancy leather interior and I loved it. It was everything I hoped it would be. That baby would go so fast and haul so much, I just felt more powerful everywhere I went. Another Durango owner once commented to me that a Durango could pass anything on the road—except a gas station. True statement.

I chose the wrong time to buy my dream car. I had just started a business and my income began to drop shortly after buying the car. It was amazing to me how the Durango failed to attract new business. Couldn't people see how powerful I was? Alas, the car had to go.

I struggled along making the payments for 18 months and then sold the car. At that point, I think I had to pay out of pocket about $1,000 to pay off the loan when I sold the car. So I sat down and figured out how much the car had cost me every month for the 18 months I'd owned it. The answer: $1,500 per month. And that was back in 2002 after buying the car in 2000 for almost $10,000 less than the example above.

So, I bought a Volvo with 314,000 miles on it for $1,300. I drove the Volvo for two years. Yes, I had to do a variety of repairs and it was not a reliable car (thank heaven for AAA). The average monthly ownership cost for the Volvo was on the order of $300. The insurance was cheaper, the gas was cheaper, the depreciation was virtually nil, the capital cost was nearly zero, and most repairs were less than $200.

So, if you have an expensive car you cannot afford, there is an old Volvo out there somewhere just waiting for you.

Before you get too anxious about what other people will think of you, let me suggest that most people don't care what you drive. Many people will like you more if you drive a less expensive car. While there are a few people who will think less of you (just being honest here), would you really want to live your life by the standard of someone who would judge your personal worth by something as superficial as the car you drive?

Now, let me clarify. If you are presently driving a car for which you paid $25,000 three years ago and you're thinking I've just suggested that you sell it and buy a brand new $20,000 car, you've misread me. In fact, I only want you to sell your car today and replace it with another car if two conditions hold: 1) you own a car you can no longer afford, and 2) you are willing to drive a clunker for at least two years while you start a savings plan to get you into shape for driving a somewhat more upscale car than a 20-year-old Volvo with 314,000 miles.

If you are like most people reading this book, your plan should simply be to keep driving the car you drive today. For a long time.

Buying and selling cars is tremendously inefficient. Not only do cars depreciate generally, it is virtually impossible for you to sell a car and get the same price a dealer would charge for the same used car. People inside the car dealership world have told me repeatedly that they essentially make all of their profits on used cars. This only works because they won't give you a fair value on your trade-in and they can sell used cars for a premium because of their location, advertising budget, reputation and repair facilities.

That means every time you trade in a car and buy a new one—even just a newer used car—you are making a giant contribution to the welfare of the car dealership. Keep that money for your cause instead! There are people starving in Africa right now, please don't go and give $5,000 of profit to a car dealer today.

Let me suggest a specific plan for your car ownership going forward. Do what you want, but let me at least suggest this for your consideration.

Keep the car you have, which most likely involves a car payment. Keep making the payments until the car is paid off. Then buy yourself a new pair of shoes to celebrate—not a new car!

Keep driving the car for at least four more years and here is the key part of the plan (pay attention to this): keep making the payment! Of course, you shouldn't send it to the bank where you've been sending the payments, put it in a savings account. Every month make the payment to your future car savings account. Within about four years you'll be in a position to take your car (it'll be pretty old by then, right?) and your savings account down to the dealership to buy a very nice, "previously owned" car for cash! Drive that car for five to seven years making payments to yourself the whole time and then return to the dealership. You'll discover by this point that your savings plus the value of the car will buy a very nice new car. Don't do it. Buy a nice previously owned car (and a new pair of shoes) and give the extra $5,000 or $10,000 to your cause and keep making the car payments to yourself every month.

If you simply must buy a new car with the money, be sure that you drive that new car for a long time. Shoot for ten years. Take very good care of it and keep making those car payments to yourself so that you can always afford to replace your car without a loan.

That car fund can also be used, heaven forbid, to fund a big repair to your car. If you lose a transmission or an engine, it is tempting to replace the car. The logic often used to justify the purchase of a new car goes something like this. My car is only worth $3,000 with the new transmission that will cost me $2,000 so I may as well just get a new car. You've certainly heard that sort of logic before. Maybe you even bought a new car using that logic. But let me be clear, you could buy a new transmission for your clunker about every two months for what a new Durango would cost you—even if you pay cash! Dip into your car savings, if need be, to keep the old car running.

Let me suggest, too, that you try to keep your car in good shape. If you wash it regularly and do all of the required maintenance when it is scheduled you'll find yourself happier with your used car. Don't let your car get so dirty and broken that you hate driving it. Treat it right and you can drive it for 100,000 miles—at least. Most cars will have no trouble getting to 150,000 with tender loving care.

If you make car payments to yourself for as long as you made them to the bank, your savings account, together with the value of your car, will almost certainly be enough to buy a new model of the same car you had before without a penny of debt. If you choose to buy a lesser car and give more to your cause instead, then you're really living your dream! That is how you can really make a mark on the world.

Now, keep reading to learn how to save money with a home!

Chapter 13

"A Culture of Giving"

When Dallin Larsen, Randy Larsen, his brother, and Henry Marsh launched what was to become one of the largest companies in the network marketing industry, MonaVie[23], they agreed that it was important to begin giving back even before they achieved notable success.

At their first meeting with distributors to launch the new juice drink that would quickly get the attention of media, the MonaVie Founders auctioned off the first case of juice for what turned out to be $5,000 and gave the money to charity.

As MonaVie grew, they turned their attention to fostering a foundation that would do something great, not just something good, in a world that desperately needed it.

Of their goals, Dallin recently explained to me, "When we started MonaVie, one of the first things we did to help create a culture of giving was to create The MORE Project where we feed, clothe and educate children living in poverty. This has enabled our distributors around the world to understand what it means to live a more meaningful life, through service to others. We teach that when you are blessed personally, it's important to become a blessing to others. Each company has a culture. We are striving to create a culture of personal responsibility and service, not because anyone is required to do so but out of love and a desire to make a difference."[24]

---

23 From September 2008 through March 2011, I worked as the Chief Financial Officer for MonaVie.

24 Email from Dallin Larsen, May 17, 2012.

After looking for a time, they found Sergio Ponce, a crusader who was working in the favelas or slums of Rio De Janeiro, Brazil. Sergio devotedly works to save the children there who were not only born into poverty, but who also face all of the hazards of an urban jungle that seems to assign little value to their lives, virtually forcing them into early careers in the drug and sex trades.

Born from this meeting, The MORE Project began its work to provide education, food and in some cases, housing, for these victimized and impoverished children, to give them an opportunity to choose a life that was not doomed to end in prison or worse.

Megan Wolfenden, MonaVie's top distributor in Australia, traveled with a group of top distributors to volunteer at The MORE Project in 2010 (I was privileged to join her on that trip). She noted, "The founders of MonaVie realised that it was their corporate and social duty to set up a foundation to give back to the country that provided so much of the raw materials for their famous and wonderful products."[25]

Rayane Ferreira Cruz and Megan Wolfenden.
Photo by Devin Thorpe.

25 Email from Megan Wolfenden, June 26, 2012.

If you ever attend a MonaVie event, you might come away with the impression that MonaVie only exists to generate money for The MORE Project. That impression would not be too far from the truth. Though MonaVie is a for-profit business that has been tremendously successful, the Founders continue to focus on the need to give back.

Founder Henry Marsh, who earned a place on four U.S. Olympic teams and set an American record in the steeple-chase, developed a passion for service and a love for the people in Brazil early in life. You see, Marsh took two years out of his intense Olympic training schedule to volunteer as a missionary for his church in Brazil; he's never lost the love for the people he developed then and remains passionate about the work of The MORE Project.

Henry says, "I've learned that serving the children of The MORE Project teaches this great life lesson: it's not what you get out of life that counts, but what you give."[26]

In keeping with the spirit of giving, Henry not only retains the ability to speak Portuguese but is also conversant in Spanish, allowing him to connect personally with people throughout Latin America.

Founder Randy Larsen, Dallin's older brother, rarely speaks about his experiences in Brazil without tearing up. In the early days of MonaVie, Randy spent a great deal of time developing the supply chain for the company's voracious appetite for acai berries, previously virtually unknown outside Brazil. What Randy saw was that the demand for the berries, which grow in a particular variety of tropical palm trees in the Amazon rainforest, was serving both to provide a livelihood for indigenous populations living at the lowest end of the economic spectrum and by doing so, that demand was serving to protect the rainforest.

Randy has insisted that the work of The MORE Project include the people and schools in the rainforest who help to supply MonaVie with the acai for its products. Over

---

26 Email from James Marsh, June 9, 2012.

the years, despite his tremendous success, Randy has spent time in the rainforest, away from any modern conveniences, sleeping with his friends at the very beginning of the supply chain, the folks who climb the trees to harvest the berries. You can see the love he has for the people in his glistening eyes whenever he talks about his experiences among them.

He notes, "One of the primary things that motivates us at MonaVie is making a difference in the lives of people all over the world."[27]

Every year, the distributors, the Founders and the Company combine to donate millions of dollars to The MORE Project and its mission. This funding has allowed the mission of The MORE Project to expand beyond the borders of Brazil.

Already, The MORE Project has responded to a variety of disasters around the world, raising money and providing support directly to organizations on the ground for such causes as Australian wildfires, the 2010 earthquake in Haiti, tsunami victims in Japan, and most recently, flood victims in Thailand. The MORE Project is working to launch ongoing efforts in Mexico, Thailand and India this year.[28]

In 2010, I took the opportunity to visit Brazil to see the operations of The MORE Project and the impact it was having. I traveled with a group of MonaVie distributors from America and Australia. As I watched them interact with the children at The MORE Project school, it was impossible to tell who was happier, the volunteers or the children.

The children, among the poorest in the world, were being educated in a beautiful, safe and modern facility with access to all the world's knowledge, loving teachers and countless supporters working to help them. When this group of distributors arrived, they were thronged by the children who literally leapt into their arms and sometimes right on top of them, climbing onto shoulders or swarming over a tackled

---

27 MonaVie Newsroom (http://newsroom.monavie.com/?page_id=225)
28 MonaVie Newsroom (http://newsroom.monavie.com/?page_id=392)

volunteer like army ants on a carcass. It absolutely pegged the happiness meter.

Dallin, Henry and Randy taught me an important lesson about giving: start giving well before you're done getting! They'll leave a remarkable mark on the world precisely because they started giving when there wasn't much to give and continued giving generously from their abundance.

The MORE Project
10855 South River Front Parkway Suite 100
South Jordan, UT 84095, USA
(801) 208-1145
Info@themoreproject.org
www.themoreproject.org

Chapter 14

Owning a Home

Home ownership may not be all that it was cracked up to be in the early half of the last decade. Then, financing was easy and everyone seemed to fall for the line that real estate was a safe investment because its value "always goes up over time." That said, owning a home in a prudent way can provide a firm base for your financial planning and it can fit in nicely with your plans to do something good, something meaningful with your life.

Over the very long haul, real estate does tend to go up in value, roughly in line with inflation. This is not true in all markets nor is it true over all "long periods" but it is generally true. When I say, "long periods," by the way, I mean mortgage long periods of time, say 15 to 30 years. Over those spans of time real estate tends to rise in value.

At the same time a home is rising in value, so are rental rates, but your mortgage payment is typically stable. Even better, that stable mortgage payment is increasingly going toward principal as the mortgage ages, so while you're still sending cash to the bank every month, more of it is effectively accruing to your benefit.

Let's consider a basic, hypothetical example to make sure that this point is clear in your mind.

If you buy a home in 2012 for $250,000 with a $50,000 down payment, you'll start with a $200,000 mortgage. If we use 4.5% as our presumptive interest rate, that would yield a principal and interest payment, a mortgage payment that is, of $1,013.37 per month. Let's assume for the moment that you could rent the same home or a comparable one for about $1,200 per month. As a homeowner, you are also responsible for more of the maintenance of the home, along with taxes and insurance so the total monthly cost to own the home might seem to be higher than the cost to rent it—but the tax deduction for the interest would likely change the math, meaning that it is likely cheaper to buy a home than to rent one.

Of course, I'm skipping the step where you somehow find $50,000 for a down payment. So, let's talk about that for a minute. Having worked in the mortgage business, I can say confidently that lots of people get help from their parents in buying a home. Not everyone, of course, and I can't provide statistics to say what percent of homebuyers get help from parents, but I can say that many do. My point is, don't be shy about asking your parents for help. I know that doesn't sound very emancipated, but the reality is that coming up with a down payment is seriously hard and you should leave no stone unturned.

Other places to look for a down payment include your retirement savings. Especially if you are in your 30's or younger, it is reasonable to use your retirement savings to buy a modest home. Don't mortgage your future by using your retirement savings to buy a big dream house that you can barely afford. It will put pressure on your budget and make surviving in retirement harder.

Let me put it this way, you are much better off being the "rich people" in the neighborhood you choose than the "poor people." If you stretch to buy a home in a neighborhood where everyone is more affluent, you will feel pressure to do a variety of things they do but that you can't afford, like summer vacations in Europe, driving a BMW and doing 100 other little things from cello lessons for the kids to expensive summer camps. If you are the rich ones in a more modest neighborhood, you'll feel the opposite pressure. Your neighbors will take more modest vacations, drive more modest cars and choose more carefully among the activities for their kids, allowing you to use your money to do the good you want to do instead of feeling a constant need to explain to your wealthy neighbors why you choose to drive an older car, or won't be vacationing in Paris this summer.

Getting back to the question of the down payment, it may make sense for a variety of reasons to sell some assets to buy a home. If you own a car with no payment and don't absolutely need the car (you could take the bus or the train to work) then you may want to consider selling the car to buy the house.

Good, old-fashioned savings are another tried and true way to save for a down payment. Here again, many parents help out their kids by allowing them to live in a basement or even in their old bedroom for a year or two while they save for the down payment. Parents, who may not have the cash to help, may have a bedroom or basement they'd contribute to the effort. I'm always amazed by the parents who allow not just a 30-year old child, but her spouse and three kids to come live with them for a year or two.

And, let me be clear, you don't need a full 20% down payment to buy a house. If you don't have that much, the mortgage lender will simply require you to buy what is called mortgage insurance. This insurance protects the lender—not you—in case you can't make your payments and the bank has to take your house. While this is depressing, this is what allows most people to buy a first home.

Some mortgage programs using Federal Housing Authority or FHA loans allow for down payments as low as three to five percent.

The monthly mortgage insurance factors in to what you can afford or qualify for in a mortgage. So if you could qualify for a $200,000 mortgage with a $50,000 down payment, you may only be able to qualify for a $190,000 mortgage with a $10,000 down payment due to the cost of the mortgage insurance.

Now, let's look at what happens 15 years after you buy a home (or don't).

The home you bought for $250,000 has appreciated at a modest rate of about three percent each year. This is principally because of the inflation in the cost to replace your home, plus a bit of real appreciation in the land your home sits on, offset by depreciation in the physical home itself. You may experience higher or lower returns, but over 15 years a three percent annual return would be reasonable. That would mean your home is worth about $389,000.

At the same time, your mortgage has been amortizing nicely and after fifteen years you owe only $132,000. When you bought the home, the mortgage was 80% of the value and now it is only 34% of the value of your home. To rent the same home 15 years from now would likely cost about $1,870 per month but the mortgage costs you only $1,013 per month, just like it did way back in 2012.

Now, I hope you can begin to see the value of a home purchase. It is not a sure fire way to get rich; it is a practical way to build financial stability over time. You'll save hundreds of dollars each month compared to renting. You'll expand your $50,000 down payment into equity of $257,000, likely making it the centerpiece of your financial plan and the bulk of your balance sheet.

The surest way to foul up this forecast is to move every three to five years. Buying and selling a home is not that different from buying and selling a car. It is inherently expensive!

If you are buying and selling in a buyer's market, when home values are soft, you'll feel real pressure to discount the price of your home in order to sell it. It will be difficult to make that up in some way on the purchase of your new home. Even worse, if you are buying in a seller's market, you'll be pressured to bid up the price of the home you want, hoping you'll be able to make that up on the sale of your own home.

On each transaction, the purchase and sale, total transaction costs will approach ten percent of the purchase price. Typically, the majority of those costs are paid by the seller from the proceeds of the sale, but keep in mind that when you are the buyer, you are providing those proceeds.

So, let's say you decide to sell your home long before the 15 years are up and your home has appreciated 10%, up to $275,000. By the time you pay all of the transaction costs for the move, you'll likely pay about $27,500, meaning that you will net $247,500—less than you paid for your house. You don't have to be a rocket scientist to figure out that selling things for less than you paid to buy them is not the quickest path to wealth.

The bottom line with home ownership is remarkably similar to the conclusions we reached about owning cars. Keep them for a long time. As a general rule, you will be better off financially to keep up and fix up your home than to sell it and buy a new one.

For those who bought or buy a home since about 2009, you may never be tempted to refinance. Mortgage rates have been quite low for several years as the Federal Reserve has made an effort to reduce long term interest rates (along with short term rates), specifically to support home values and spur long term corporate investments.

But, for those who bought homes previously and borrowed money at rates above five percent, there will be a temptation to refinance the mortgage. If you are willing to follow my advice to stay in your home for a long time, it makes sense to refinance if you can accomplish two goals: 1) reduce the interest rate by at least one full percentage point, and 2) reduce the term of the mortgage.

Note that I did not make reducing the payment one of the criteria for the refinance. In fact, if you shorten the term of the loan, you may increase your mortgage payment. Since you first bought your home several years ago, however, you may have had an increase in income that would support a higher payment so it may make a lot of sense to refinance to get a higher payment—with a lower interest rate and much more money going to principal.

Note that some financial advisors suggest never retiring your mortgage because the after-tax cost of mortgage financing is so low. They are right about the math, but they ignore the peaceful feeling you get from knowing that you own your own home, free and clear of any encumbrance. It also provides you with a dramatically increased ability to do good in the world. If you have no mortgage, you are empowered with real leverage to go out and make a difference.

If you refinance your mortgage, your loan officer will likely suggest that you consider borrowing some extra money to pay off consumer debt or to make home improvements.

Using mortgage money, even with a 15 or 20 year mortgage (which is relatively short, compared to the standard 30 year mortgage) to pay for your summer vacation in Italy or to pay off your car (that will be in the scrap heap long before you make the final payment) is an unsound way to free up cash flow now. That will simply mean you are potentially trapping yourself in your job as you approach retirement, when you might rather retire a year or two early and take some time while you are still young and healthy to volunteer for your cause.

If you must finance a car or other consumer purchase, it is best to let those payments provide the discipline they should, by forcing you to get them paid off in a time that corresponds to the useful life (or less) of the item purchased. Those stiff monthly payments should inspire you to save for the next purchase rather than enslaving you in debt. Debt, and especially consumer debt, binds you to your employment and saps the joy of working precisely because you have no choice. It also wipes out your ability to leave your mark on the world.

We'll talk more about how to manage and get out of debt so keep reading!

Chapter 15

Optimism from Despair

The first sign that something was wrong came during the final weeks of Alta's pregnancy; the baby was not growing. When she delivered the baby late in 2007, everyone was relieved to see the tiny, five-pound baby Elliot with all his fingers and toes and apparently doing well. Their relief would not last long.[29]

Within a month, it was apparent that Elliot was not thriving. Even after repeated visits to the pediatrician the six-week old baby still weighed just five pounds. After three months their pediatrician sent them to a specialist. After he ran some tests, Mike and Alta got a late Friday night call that would change their lives. Elliot had cystic fibrosis or CF.

CF is a genetic disorder that affects the lungs as well as the intestines, pancreas, and liver. Those affected by the disease lack enzymes that play a key role in clearing lungs of naturally occurring mucus and for digesting food, hence Elliot's failure to grow. No matter how much he was fed, he simply could not derive enough nutrition from the food to grow.

As the extended family got the news and began to gather in support of the family lots of tears were shed and prayers were offered. Elliot's grandfather, Richard (Rick) Davis, left his daughter's home and went straight to his computer to begin searching the internet for information about CF. Of the experience, he says now, "Nothing I found was good. Eve-

---

29   Richard Davis provided this information in a phone interview on May 11, 2012, and in additional email exchanges.

rything said this was a terminal disease with no known cure."

One of the sites he found was the Cystic Fibrosis Foundation website (www.cff.org) where he signed up for the newsletter and clicked a box—without giving it much thought—indicating that he was willing to get involved.

The following Monday, Rick got a call from the executive director of the CFF Utah-Idaho Chapter asking if he was willing to meet to discuss how he might get involved; he agreed. By the end of the week, Rick, a prominent attorney in Salt Lake City, was selected to sit on the board of directors for the Utah-Idaho CFF Chapter (UI-CFF), which he now chairs.

Just three weeks after Elliot was born, his cousin Clare was born. She was born without any apparent problems and though she was a docile baby, she seemed healthy until about a year after her birth, she caught a cold and could not shake it for several months. When her pediatrician learned that Clare had a cousin with CF, the light went on, tests were run and a second CF diagnosis in the family was made.

Rick, Elliot, Clare, Alta and Grandpa Rick.
Courtesy of Richard Davis.

Rick has devoted himself to this cause with the passion and enthusiasm of a man racing against a clock that absent his personal effort would have him attend not just one but perhaps two of his grandchildren's funerals. Over the years since the first diagnosis, however, Rick has learned that there is a great deal of hope for CF patients.

As Rick rallied family and friends to the cause, the sense of tragedy that befell them began to ease. The family—always close—pulled together as never before. Everyone chipped in to help with fundraising, child rearing or the seemingly endless treatments. CF patients require nebulizer treatments and chest percussion treatments delivered through a vest twice or more each day. Each treatment can take an hour. The work alone is never ending.

As the family pulled together, they began to look at the disease as a blessing. They recognized that with a large extended family, good jobs and good health insurance, they were in the perfect place to care for these kids and that the challenge brought them all closer.

Rick began attending national CFF conferences regularly where reasons for therapeutic optimism are shared. Following a CFF conference in Bethesda, he attended an event-planning meeting in Ogden, Utah where he met a single mother of a six-year-old CF patient. The mother, despondent herself, was planning to leave the conference early to get home to her boy who had told her he was so miserable and tired of the persistent hospitalizations he just wanted to "go back to Jesus."

This painful experience helped Rick to recognize that not every family impacted by CF has the same resources, the same economic and social situation. For some it would seem simply too much too handle. He began to appreciate that CF "is a rich man's disease" but that not everyone impacted by it is rich. Clare's parents were having to pay $20,000 per year out of pocket—with health insurance. They have changed his job twice to find employers with more generous health insurance plans. Furthermore, even for those whose pocket books are adequate, the caregiving stress without an extended network is still overwhelming.

Through the local CF clinic and an active parents' group, a great effort is now being made to ensure that all CF patients gets access to the necessary treatments, regardless of their financial situation. For those with financial limitations there are a variety of programs available to help cover the almost infinite costs. Recently, the UI-CFF parents' group has expanded, supplementing the self-help group focused on sharing members' problems, with much-appreciated social functions so that parents not only share their problems but also their joys and their progress.

News in the CF world has been increasingly good since 2008. Early in 2012, an exciting new drug, Kalydeco, was introduced; it treats just a small fraction of CF patients—perhaps only 1,000 people in the U.S. But treat CF it does. One 24-year-old patient that Rick described had to quit singing and running in high school and could no longer even walk up stairs. On the new drug, within weeks she felt better and now can walk up stairs again and sings like an angel. "We are on the cusp of seeing a dramatic change," Rick says regarding the treatment of CF, with new drugs in the pipeline.

In order to increase funding, Rick worked to expand the size of the UI-CFF board of directors from six to fifteen members. He's also worked to add more people who are not parents of CF patients—parents have enough to worry about. By drawing on the larger community and Rick's personal network of well-heeled attorneys and other professionals in the community, the exposure of the organization and its success have dramatically increased.

Since Rick joined the board in 2008, the UI-CFF revenue has more than doubled. At the 2011 edition of the gala—Taste of Utah—the UI-CFF generated more revenue than the organization generated in all of 2008. Last year, the chapter even won an award from the national organization for having the largest increase in revenue year over year for its market size.

Rick explained the dramatic change in CF treatment over the years this way: In 1950, a CF diagnosis usually meant that a child had just a few years to live. By 1980, a CF diagnosis typically meant a child could likely attend high school but would not likely be at graduation. A CF patient born today—much like a diabetic—is likely to live long enough to die from something else.

This also means that Rick can expect to have all of his grandchildren attend his funeral to celebrate the mark he left on the world.

Cystic Fibrosis Foundation
Utah and Idaho Chapter
124 South 400 East
Suite 250
Salt Lake City, UT 84111
p: (801) 532-2335
Email: utah@cff.org
www.cff.org

Chapter 16

Eliminate the Trolls

There is nothing more futile than wanting to give more to your cause and knowing you can't because little debt trolls won't let you.

My generation grew up believing that it was important to establish a good credit rating by borrowing some money and then repaying it. Many of us established very good credit with an emphasis on borrowing money and then making regular payments toward its satisfaction.

In fact, until the recent economic debacle caused by overloads of debt, which led to regulatory and market changes in consumer debt, it wasn't unusual for credit cards to have such small minimum payments that one would literally be able to stretch a $10,000 balance over 30 years (in part, because the payment would decline a tiny bit each month, but mostly because so little principle was required in the first place).

Most of those younger than I got their first credit cards as a right of passage when they started college. College bookstores seemed for a time to be more about helping students get into debt than about getting them their books!

Hence, we've grown up, you and I, in a world of easy credit and a culture that values conspicuous consumption over inconspicuous savings.

The truth is that every debt we have brings with it a little troll who gets to tell us what we can and can't do.

Most people readily invite a mortgage troll into their homes because without him, there would be no home. Makes good sense.

Some also have a troll or two sitting in the living room representing the cars in the garage.

Others, in addition to the mortgage troll and the car loan trolls, also have trolls for their college diplomas, despite the fact they can't sell the diplomas to anyone else no matter how nicely framed they are.

Still, others have, in addition to all of these trolls, a whole party room full of trolls. The Visa, MasterCard and American Express trolls are shooting pool in the basement while the department store trolls dance on their furniture.

There is no more a healthy amount of debt than there is a healthy amount of cancer. The difference is that we need some debt to get us started, but we should be as focused on evicting the trolls from our lives as we would be about removing cancer if we had it.

This is especially true for you. Above all, you want to give more and do more for your cause. You can't do it if you have debt trolls living in every room of your house with you. They'll always be there to say, "You can't give more to your cause because you need to feed me. Feed me! FEED ME!!!"

So let's talk about how to get rid of the trolls. This will take time and it starts with a simple principle: stop borrowing more money.

This sounds easy, but is hard. Let's do a quick assessment.

Make a list of all of your debts. Every single one of them.

If you can, set up a spreadsheet with four columns:

1. Lender/Issuer
2. Current balance
3. Monthly payment
4. Interest rate

Note that if you don't own a home but rent, you should include your rent as a monthly payment.

In a spreadsheet you can quickly sort these by any of the four columns, to rank these in priority alphabetically (meaningless), by size, by monthly cash impact, or by their relative cost.

The first thing to do is to compare the total monthly cost of the debt to your total monthly income. Divide the total of the payments by your gross monthly income to determine the percentage of your income going to the trolls. There is a limit to how much money you can use each month to feed the trolls. If they want more than 40% of your income, you are almost certainly forced to borrow some of the money you give to the trolls every month. If that is where you are, you know you are out of control and the trolls have you.

If your credit is still pretty good and the trolls have you, it likely means that they haven't had you for long and you need a plan to quickly get out of trouble.

No one likes it when the trolls are in charge. Life is miserable. Let's see if we can at least banish them to the basement. There are several tactics we can use to do that.

Sell Something

If you look at the list of debts, some of the loans will be associated with an asset, something you still have that has value and that you can touch and feel—and sell. This could be anything from the car you drive, to the boat parked alongside the house or that $2,000 pool table the credit card trolls were using a few minutes ago. Your goal in this exercise is to find an asset that you can sell quickly that will reduce the total of your monthly debt payment as a percentage of your income to less than 40%.

You have to be honest with yourself and with your family about the situation. It may have made all the sense in the world to buy the boat last summer, but you may not have appreciated then how demanding the debt troll would be. If you sell the boat and send the boat troll packing, will that bring your monthly debts under the 40% target? If no single asset is big enough to make a difference, are there a collection of things that might sell well on eBay that could make a dent in the monthly numbers?

Consolidation

Once you have exhausted all the options for selling assets to reduce the debt, you may consider your consolidation options, but only after you take an honest inventory and consider selling anything that can help you get your debts back into line.

Let me put this into perspective for you this way. My wife and I once sold our home to help us get our monthly number back into line. We did this before we created any credit problems for ourselves. Lots of people do this. If you have to do it, I promise, the world won't end.

Debt consolidation is not your first plan of attack—it is the back up plan. This is your plan B. If you haven't worked on selling some assets, go back to plan A. You're not ready for plan B.

Now, if you're really ready for plan B because, for instance, there isn't enough equity in your home, the cars aren't the problem and the garage sale last weekend didn't get you over the finish line, then you may now proceed.

Depending upon the size of your problem, plan B may be very easy. If you have several credit cards with balances and one of them has additional credit available on better terms, at least a lower monthly payment, you may be able to simply transfer the balances from the other cards to the one with the easier payment schedule. Remember, though, you're just trading cute little trolls with little squeaky voices for a big mean troll with a loud voice who probably spills on the carpet. You may be worse off by virtue of this consolidation because you'll be paying on the debt longer than you had planned.

If you can't get there using the credit already available to you, you'll want to seek new credit. If you have bad credit, you may need to move to plan C. Let's hope you don't have to go there.

The most affordable source of cash for consolidation will likely be some form of home loan. If you can get your monthly debt below 40% using a second mortgage or home equity line of credit, I would recommend doing that before refinancing your first mortgage—unless you can reduce your first mortgage interest rate quite a bit or your problem is otherwise too big. Remember, when you consolidate your credit cards into a mortgage loan, you basically choose to pay interest on the dinner you ate last week for thirty years. This should be a last resort.

Work it out with the Trolls

If you can't consolidate the debt (this could easily be the case if you have poor credit or if you have little or no equity in your home), you may need to simply start working it out with the trolls—this is plan C.

In recent years, mortgage companies have started offering loan modifications. Unlike a refinance, in these cases they are simply changing the loan terms to make your payments more affordable. Banks are more willing to do so when you can demonstrate a hardship and the value of your home is below the loan balance. They now recognize there isn't much choice for them but to work with you.

Another option is to work with a consumer credit counseling agency to help you. Not-for-profit consumer counseling agencies have the legal ability to force your consumer lenders to accept a lower interest rate and payments on your consumer debt. This is not a panacea. The trolls see this as being little different from a bankruptcy and your credit will be impacted.

If one of your trolls is a student loan that cannot be discharged in bankruptcy, you can generally request a hardship forbearance for up to one year. Check with your lender. That may give you enough time to change other financial conditions to allow you to get your loans below 40%.

Finally, bankruptcy is an option. This is simply a way of getting the legal system to help you negotiate with the trolls. No one but the lawyers win in bankruptcy so I recommend that you avoid it at all costs, but

I recognize that sometimes there is no real alternative. Bankruptcy can give a fresh start. If you find yourself here, be sure to avoid mistakes that may have led you to this place.

Kicking the Trolls Out!

Once you have your monthly debt service below 40% of your gross monthly income you are ready to start kicking the trolls out!

Get your list of debts ready and sort it either by balance or by interest rate such that the loan with either the smallest balance or the highest interest rate is on top and the rest line up below it.

If you choose to work in order of interest rate, you will actually be able to pay off your debts more quickly than if you use the balance approach, but using the balance approach may be more fun, so I'll let you choose.

Once you have your sort done you'll likely see a department store credit card at the top of the list with a relatively small balance and a high interest rate—if you have one. If not, it will likely be a bank card—if you have one. In any case, the troll at the top of the list is the first one you'll kick out.

Let's assume for a moment that it is a department store card with a $1,000 balance, a 24% interest rate, and a minimum monthly payment of $50 (half of which goes to cover the interest).

Now you are going to figure out how much extra you can pay each month toward ridding yourself of trolls. It should be at least 1% of your gross monthly income but you may want to give it even more.

Here's why: if you can reduce a debt that is costing you 24% interest, that is the same as earning a 24% return on your investment—guaranteed. Once you pay off the debt, it costs you nothing, but until you do it costs you 24%. Many of you are saying, but my highest interest rate is only 12.9% or 8.9% or some such thing. There is no other investment opportunity in the world that can offer you a guaranteed return of even 8.9% today. Shaky European government bonds yield only about 7% and who knows what the guarantee is worth. What I'm saying is that if you can reduce your debts even if they aren't costing you much, you get the benefit of guaranteed returns that are far in excess of returns on cash and near cash investments.

So, let's assume that you decide you can kick in an extra $100 per month to reduce your debts. You'll apply that to your department store credit card each month—along with the $50 that is scheduled. Even if the required payment goes down, make the full $150 payment each month until it is paid off. It will take only about 8 months to pay off that loan in full. If you instead made the declining minimum monthly payment on that loan, you'd be paying 24% interest for years!

For all of your credit cards, make a note of the current monthly payment required and make that payment each month, even if the required payment goes down.

Once you have paid off the department store card with the $1,000 balance at 24% interest, you'll have an extra $150 to put toward the next debt on the list. Let's assume for a moment it's a bankcard with a $2,500 balance, an interest rate of 12.9% and a payment of $125. By applying the $150 to the $125 payment, you'll more than double the payment and dramatically increase the amount of principal paid each month. You'll be able to pay that loan off in a year!

Then, you'll have an extra $275 dollars to put toward the next loan. That one may be a big one like a student loan or a car loan, but the same principle that applied with the little loans will work with the big ones. Extra principal payments will quickly reduce the balance, reducing the interest expense and accelerating the payoff. Pretty soon you'll have kicked all the trolls out of the house except for the mortgage and then you can put the screws to the mortgage troll and kick him out of the house.

Most people find they can pay off 100% of their debts, including the mortgage within 10 to 15 years using this plan. Just think, your home can be troll free while you are still young enough to enjoy it!

Chapter 17

It Wasn't The Rats

Though it meant sliding his bare feet through their droppings, Alex Budak was careful not to lift his feet at all as he shuffled through the Temple of Rats[30] where the rodents are not only tolerated but revered, fed and sheltered right in the temple, as he preferred the droppings to stepping on a rat—which would surely have been viewed as bad form. The rats did not return the favor, scurrying over his feet as often as around them.[31]

Alex Budak. Courtesy of Alex Budak.

---

30 Wikipedia, "Karni Mata," (http://en.wikipedia.org/wiki/Karni_Mata)
31 Much of the information in this chapter not directly related to my own StartSomeGood campaign came from an interview with Alex Budak on March 21, 2012 and related email exchanges.

The rat temple provided a vivid memory of his months in India, but it wasn't actually the rats that inspired him. While in India he recognized deeper poverty than he'd seen at any time, any where in his life. He came away with the distinct impression that the world's seemingly overwhelming problems could not be addressed by a few mammoth, well-funded and well-meaning organizations, but rather required the efforts of countless small organizations, each tackling a part of the problem in its own way.

Alex explained, "I realized while in India that substantive social change won't come from one or two organizations, but rather from lots of change-makers around the world pursuing their own version of social good."

After returning from India, Alex met Tom Dawkins, while working at Ashoka, a charitable organization that sponsors "social entrepreneurs," leading social change-makers that it describes as the "Steve Jobses of the citizen sector." Tom would ultimately become his business partner.

Alex cultivated and nurtured the ideas that germinated in India with Tom. "After lots of brainstorming and (too much) coffee with my co-founder, Tom, the concept for StartSomeGood arose," Alex said. StartSomeGood would become a crowdfunding, or as Alex likes to call it, a "peer-funding" platform with the goal of catalyzing ventures that would tackle social problems in infinite ways.

Together, Alex and Tom launched StartSomeGood.com in March of 2011. Since then, the platform has been successfully used by dozens of ventures to launch their social projects. Some of the people, who raise money on the site, do so in order to fund a one-time project. Some people use it to fund the start-up of a social venture, one that has a clear social mission with a for-profit business model. Still others are charitable organizations that are raising money for a specific project.

Typically, each organization will raise a few thousand dollars, but the high-water mark was recently set by the "Do

Good Bus Tour." The popular band Foster the People organized a bus tour to accompany their concert tour. Everywhere they went along a route of nearly 10,000 miles around the country, a bus loaded with fans followed and at each of 22 stops, everyone tackled a service project like serving food in a soup kitchen, gardening, providing music education, helping at-risk-youth, or whatever project they could find. Their campaign raised a total of $101,781.

My interest in StartSomeGood ran parallel paths. When I encountered the StartSomeGood blog (StartSomeGood. tumblr.com) I was immediately intrigued. The first thing I did after reviewing the site was to submit an application. It was purely a whim and I doubted anything would come of it.

What surprised me was that I quickly received a personal email from Alex. I immediately recognized his name as the founder (from my quick survey of the site) and shot him back a note to confirm his identity, to which he immediately responded. I asked him for an interview and we quickly scheduled one.

In the meantime, I began working to update my application to meet the StartSomeGood quality standard (clearly Alex recognized that my initial application was created on a whim). After a few iterations, Alex approved my application and I was allowed to move forward to create a campaign.

For the campaign, StartSomeGood requires a video. While I love photography, I've learned over the years to really despise video, so for me this was a real project. One of the stories in this book covers the round-the-world service tour of the Smith family I met in Cambodia in January. It was meeting them that inspired me to write this book. So, with their permission, I used their photos from their blog to create a video and then created a narration about the Smiths and this book. (With my campaign now complete, I note that the video was viewed 56 times.)

Ultimately, Alex had me revise my campaign four times—each time significantly—to create something that would be appealing to site users. Alex, as you would find obvious, doesn't work from intuition about what works, but approaches it from their significant experience. He gave me great suggestions that really helped me to craft a campaign that would work.

The biggest issue was to develop a set of tiered rewards that worked both for StartSomeGood and for me. Financial support for the book would not be tax deductible, so I wanted to be sure to provide real value in exchange for the support so that supporters would not feel they needed the tax deduction.

The logic of the $5 donation was easy as I planned to sell digital copies of the book for about $5, so I agreed to provide a digital copy of the book and to include the supporters' names and the names of their chosen causes in my book. To me it seemed that it was clearly a better deal to pay the $5 and get not only the book, but your name in it—along with a mention of your cause—than to wait for the book to come out and pay $5 for a copy of the book without your name in it.

Beyond that step, however, it was challenging for me to find ways to create value for the supporters. Alex walked me through ideas that allowed me to feel like in each case we'd created a fair value exchange for the gifts. As donations increased in size, the principal benefit was increased exposure in the book for the supporters' causes. Although we scheduled rewards for people donating up to $500, the largest donation we received was at the $100 level. Three supporters contributed $100 or more; their names, plus their causes, are listed with the URLs for their causes, plus a "tweet length" plug for the causes in the acknowledgements, plus an autographed copy of the printed book, plus a digital copy of the book, plus a personal visit to any group they choose to assemble to hear it.

The most exciting part of the campaign was that I pledged to write a chapter about the cause that was most popular among the donors. That would effectively encourage people to organize a campaign to support my campaign in order to get attention in the book.

With the campaign polished and launched, I quickly began to learn what Alex meant by "peerfunding." All of the money raised came through my network. Don't get me wrong, there were a number of donors who I didn't know before the campaign started, but they were friends of my friends and family.

For the first three weeks of the campaign, no one caught on to the idea of organizing their group to pledge support for their cause in the book. In the final week, however, that changed. Becky Mitchell, a passionate professor at Nanjing University who teaches a class on community service and another on global legacies (think Ghandi, Mother Teresa, and Nelson Mandela) wanted to call attention to the things her students were doing in China. She got her friends and family to join the campaign and now you can read about the great things her students are doing in Chapter 21.

One interesting artifact of the campaign was that I received one unusually large pledge of $2,100 from a sweet, well-meaning girl in Canada that was not part of my network. She found the StartSomeGood site and pledged that amount to three campaigns. Ultimately, however, she was unable to fund her well-intentioned pledge.

In the end, the campaign raised about $800. That covered all of the costs of getting the book published plus the travel costs to visit Nanjing (from Guangzhou).

More importantly, the campaign helped me to get some exposure for the book and even more important than that, it helped me find some great stories that I would otherwise have missed. My network grew and the quality of the book was improved by the experience.

I'm grateful that Alex's time in India inspired him to create StartSomeGood so that others can get the start they need to leave a mark on the world.

StartSomeGood
(650) 678-3569
Twitter: @StartSomeGood
hello@startsomegood.com
startsomegood.com

Chapter 18

Funding Your Children's College Education

If you have no children and no plan to have any, you should skip ahead to the next chapter!

Congratulations! I presume that because you are still reading you have children whom you plan to send to college. In keeping with the view that a key tenet of being helpful to others is being careful to avoid becoming a cause ourselves, we want our children to get a good education so that they can become independent, productive members of society.

Your example of service, alongside your career, will benefit them as they seek to find meaning and purpose in life. Your focus on giving won't end with you; your children will continue the legacy, following in your footsteps. It will be much easier for your children to brag about your efforts to help orphans in China or protect the rainforest than for their friends to brag about their parent's conspicuous spending. Make them proud!

The reality is, of course, that a college education is remarkably expensive! Paying for a quality education requires planning and organization.

There are a variety of approaches that parents reasonably use to help their students through college, ranging from allowing your students to live at home with free room and board while they attend the local college to financing the whole enchilada at an Ivy League university. What you choose will likely be influenced by a variety of factors from your income to your students' performance in school and the effort they make to prepare themselves for college.

There are virtually no wrong answers to the question, "how do you help your children pay for college?" In many places, a community college education may be entirely funded by tax credits available to you or your student (depending upon who is paying the bill). In no case, however, should you conclude that you cannot afford to send your kids to college.

Several of the best universities in the world, including Harvard and Princeton, will provide your children with a free education—including room and board—if your household income is below a given threshold (Harvard's is $65,000 in 2012.) For families with modest incomes (for 2012, anything below $150,000 but above $65,000) the costs are discounted and help in obtaining financial aid are also provided.

While I've said that there is no right or wrong plan for helping your students, let me suggest a specific plan anyway. My point is only to help you determine how much money you really should be saving each month for your students' college education.

What I'd propose is that you choose the school to which you are willing to pay the tuition and either, assume that your kids will live at home while in school, or that they will be responsible for their own room and board (not a ridiculous suggestion).

For the sake of a starting point, let's assume for a moment that you want your student to go to Harvard and you expect to have the financial obligation to pay the full tuition bill (you will be too well off for the discounted tuition formula—congratulations!). The following table sets out the monthly savings required starting today in 2012 for a student who will be admitted in the year indicated.

Saving Plan for Harvard (Estimated Costs)			
Year Student Starts College	Annual Cost	Total Cost	Monthly Savings Required
2012	$36,305	$151,804	$3,040
2013	$37,394	$156,358	$2,480
2014	$38,516	$161,049	$2,107
2015	$39,671	$165,880	$1,841
2016	$40,862	$170,856	$1,643
2017	$42,087	$175,982	$1,489
2018	$43,350	$181,262	$1,366
2019	$44,651	$186,699	$1,266
2020	$45,990	$192,300	$1,183
2021	$47,370	$198,069	$1,113
2022	$48,791	$204,011	$1,053
2023	$50,255	$210,132	$1,002

2024	$51,762	$216,436	$957
2025	$53,315	$222,929	$918
2026	$54,915	$229,617	$884
2027	$56,562	$236,505	$854
2028	$58,259	$243,600	$826
2029	$60,007	$250,908	$802
2030	$61,807	$258,436	$780
2031	$63,661	$266,189	$760
2032	$65,571	$274,174	$743

The table assumes that your investments will earn an average of just 2% over the years; while I hope you do much better, in today's economic environment anything that would yield more than that would have some risk attached that you may not like. Furthermore, I've assumed a 3% inflation rate for Harvard's tuition. That is well below the inflation rate for Harvard tuition over the last generation. The monthly savings required would vary dramatically if you changed those assumptions. For simplicity, may I suggest you think of it this way; if you end up saving too much, you'll have that much extra to give to your cause and if you end up saving too little, you'll be much better prepared than most despite the gap. The university will help you figure out how to close the gap. Finally, let's hope this formula yields the right amount (don't be afraid to save a little more if you can).

If you are like me, you look at these numbers and think, "holy cow!" So, you may want to think about saving up for a school that would be less expensive than Harvard. The following table compares the in-state (where applicable) tuition at various schools to the Harvard tuition to give you a guide as to how you might adjust your savings plan.

Cost of Tuition Relative to Harvard		
School	Annual Tuition	Relative to Harvard
University of Utah	$6,474	18%
University of North Carolina at Chapel Hill	$7,008	19%
University of Texas at Austin	$10,326	28%
University of Michigan at Ann Arbor	$14,246	39%
University of California at Berkeley	$14,461	40%
University of Southern California	$42,818	118%

Let's hope this table helps you to feel a bit better about the situation. So, if you would like to send your student to the University of North Carolina at Chapel Hill, you only need to save 19% as much as if you were going to send your student to Harvard. UNC is a fine school and you could certainly tell your student to pay the difference herself if she really wants to go to Harvard instead of UNC.

To be clear about the meaning here, if your future college student is an infant today and will be enrolling in 2032 and you are planning to send her to UNC, you'd need to save $143 each month, which you calculated by finding the savings requirement from the Harvard table and the percentage from the Harvard comparison table ($743 x 19%). It is still a lot of money, but it is radically better than trying to fund college without the benefit of college savings!

Don't forget to explore every possible scholarship available to you. Most universities have a long list of scholarships that are available, some of which go to the student who happens to apply for it. Many scholarships are established by individuals with a specific philanthropic goal. Perhaps they want to help students who attended their old high school, or who come from the same small town or the same country. As a result, a rather ordinary student who meets the target criteria will generally be given the scholarship ahead of more qualified students who don't fit the unique target, so be sure to check with the financial aid office for all of the available scholarships for which your student can apply.

Keep in mind that there are a variety of tax credits intended to help students pay for college. These tax credits won't cover the cost of tuition at Harvard, but the tax credits are large enough for many working families to cover the cost of attending a local community college—and in some cases, it may be enough to cover most of the cost of a four-year education.

The American Opportunity Tax Credit: This program provides a tax credit of $2,500 for two-parent families with a household income of up to $160,000. This means that if your income is below the threshold, you will get back up to $2,500 of the taxes you paid on a dollar for dollar basis for every dollar you spent on qualifying educational expenses. You can get this credit for up to four years for each of your students, even if they are in school at the same time! Even better news is that if you don't pay much in tax because of your generous charitable contributions and your personal exemptions for having lots of dependents and such, you can still get up to $1,000 per student back each year. In other words, even if you pay no tax, the federal government will chip in $1,000 toward each of your students' education for the first four years each one is in school.

The Lifelong Learning Credit: This credit provides a 20% tax credit of up to $1,000 for $5,000 of qualified education expenses. This tax credit is not limited to the first four years of post-secondary education, but it is limited to one credit per tax return, so you can't get this tax credit for two or more children at one time.

In addition to these tax credits, other provisions in the tax code are designed to help as well. Withdrawals from a traditional IRA would normally be subject to a penalty, but for qualified educational expenses, no penalty applies (though you still have to pay tax on the withdrawal).

Be sure to talk to your tax advisor about which of these tax credits may apply to you in your situation—and to look for other less common tax helps for which you may be eligible.

Finally, let me offer a word of caution about borrowing money to pay for your children's tuition. Education is a bit like starting a business. You don't know how much it will be worth in the future. Of course, we know that education is very important and that opportunities expand dramatically because of a quality education, but the bottom line is that you won't know how much you or your student will earn in the future and you cannot give the education back and ask for a refund. You can't sell that Harvard diploma two years after graduation to pay off the student loans if you decide you don't want to keep making the payments.

If you were to borrow all of the eligible expenses for a Harvard education today, the total loan would be on the order of $250,000—which buys an average size home in most of the country. That is a tremendous amount of debt to saddle yourself or your student with.

Again, thinking about education like a business, most banks would require that you have a lot of equity invested in a new business before they would lend you any money for it. You should approach education much the same way—even though the banks don't!

If you are carefully funding your children's education with savings, scholarships and tax credits, it may make sense for you or your student to borrow enough to enable your children to go to college. Student loans should be the tip of the pyramid, if you will, not the foundation. The foundation should be money that never has to be repaid—your savings, scholarships and tax credits.

If you use this approach to finance your students education, you'll make sure that you are not over extending yourself and as a result you'll be able to continue giving to your cause and making the difference in the world that you—and your children—want you to make!

Chapter 19

A Long Time Coming

Mark began planning for this year when he was 18 years old. It was about seeing the world, yes, but more than that, it was about volunteering to help somewhere. He talks about his planning in a humble, matter-of-fact way. He doesn't seem to appreciate how remarkable he is or the difference he is making in the world.[32]

Raised in Wisconsin, Mark Rippel was eager to expand his horizons, so for 30 years he built a career and saved. And he saved. While I didn't pin him down, he made it clear he isn't worried about the money running out.

Mark Rippel. Photo by Devin Thorpe.

32 I interviewed Mark in Cambodia on April 21, 2012 at the PSE School, where he gave me a tour of the bakery and the school campus.

When Mark approached his employer about leaving to do a year or two of service-focused world travel, he expected simply to quit his job. His employer, Swiss Tek Coating, suggested he take an indefinite leave of absence instead.

In Mark's particular circumstance, he decided to sell his home because he was doubtful the home's value would be stable while he was gone for so long and he didn't want to worry about his home for the whole time he was gone.

Mark's first volunteer effort was in South Africa, placed through African Impact. There, he worked with medically trained personnel (Mark is not medically trained) to help and assist people who were too ill to travel on their own for medical care. The volunteers helped to shuttle people back and forth to care centers. AIDS patients, for instance, are required to appear in person to get their monthly prescription, regardless of how sick they may—or may not—be.

Mark found a highlight in the intimacy of helping people who were near death. Many of the patients had to be carried from place to place. Generally, family members carried the patients. Many were in such pain that they moaned with every step. After a time, as Mark got to know some of the patients, they allowed him—with his strong, tall frame—to carry them.

He specifically recalled the significance of the moment when carrying a particularly feeble patient, that the man grabbed Mark's shirt in back and clung desperately to it, holding on to Mark as he carried him. The man died within a day or two. Mark takes pride, however, in having delivered him to his caregivers in such a personal way, giving this dying man a sense of being loved and cared for as he approached death.

While in Africa, Mark researched his next volunteer opportunity on the internet and found UBELONG, a social venture founded by two international development professionals, Cedric Hodgeman and Raul Roman, who met at Cornell University. UBELONG places volunteers in two to 24 week volunteer positions in countries where there is great need. UBELONG also organizes international development expeditions.

Through UBELONG he volunteered at a French-sponsored NGO in Phnom Penh, Cambodia, where I visited with Mark.

Pour Un Sourire d'Enfant (PSE) began with a French couple that was shocked by seeing children scavenging for food in the dump. Having seen that, they felt they could no longer do nothing. They created a school for the children and even compensate the families of the children; in their impoverished circumstances, children like these who are not in school are expected by their families to generate income—mostly by scavenging.

The school now starts with pre-school age children, allowing parents to be more productive in their efforts to provide, stretching all the way through post-secondary vocational training. Students who are behind are pushed to complete two academic years each calendar year, giving more the potential to attend college. Altogether, there are about 2,000 students in the various programs today.

Those who can't go on to college are provided with post-secondary vocational training, mostly focused on the tourist industry. The students all receive some English training to help them succeed in the country's largest industry.

Among the vocational programs at the school is a baking and pastry program where Mark volunteers. He draws upon 15 years of baking experience (gained prior to his ten years at Swiss Tek Coatings), allowing Mark to leverage his skills to help the students. He serves as an assistant to the teacher (all of the staff members are Cambodian) who teaches in the program.

Mark lives with a host family. The family lives on the main floor of their home, which has four bedrooms plus a bathroom on the second floor where up to four volunteers live. The family has a rapidly rotating group of up to four volunteers there; Mark's twelve weeks will be a relatively long stay in their home.

He is happy with the arrangement and noted that his host has been very gracious. He bought a bike, with coaching from his host, and can now navigate about the city on his own.

Mark got a flat tire one day on the way home. The next day, after an unusually long day at school, he dreaded the task of having to repair the bike that evening but discovered his host had taken care of it for him. The family provides all of Mark's meals, though he often eats at school rather than at home due to his schedule.

Mark's day starts early at the school, with classes beginning at 6:30 a.m. They operate a real bakery to support the cafeteria for the students, a restaurant in the small hotel operated on campus, and for a fine dining restaurant in the city, operated by PSE (where I can attest to the food being outstanding and the service being even better, with prices that were modest—even by Phnom Penh standards).

Mark related a moment when he watched the sea of students moving about campus one morning that he commented to one of the teachers, "I bet the founders are proud of what they've done here," to which the teacher responded, "I'm proud, too."

Mark and I agreed that he should be proud, too.

Already, he's thinking about the next opportunity. He's not sure where in the world he'll go or what he'll do, but in Mark's quiet and unassuming way, he'll leave yet another mark on the world.

African Impact
www.africanimpact.com
1-800-606-7185
17 Carlton Close
Sunnydale
Noordhoek

Cape Peninsula
Western Cape
South Africa

UBELONG
www.ubelong.org
1 202 250 3706
1630 R Street NW, Suite 5
Washington, DC 20009 USA

Pour un Sourire d'Enfant
www.pse.asso.fr
01 39 67 17 25 (France)
19, rue Lamartine
78035 VERSAILLES
France

Chapter 20

Insuring Your Plan

You can't be the solution to any problem if you are a problem. Everyone has problems and most of us will have problems that we could not survive if we didn't have good insurance.

Insurance is a complex arena that requires practitioners to obtain special licenses. Because of the complexity, very few insurance agents handle all of the insurance you need, so you'll likely be talking to several people. In addition to the insurance experts you choose, I would encourage you to bounce your thoughts off some other financial expert to help you balance the information you get from the insurance folks who make their living selling insurance.

Most people do not seem to me to have enough insurance. Insurance is expensive and for most things, it seems that we can get along just fine most days without it. The problem is that every day is not most days. Some days we need insurance.

It is well beyond the scope of this book to cover all of the information you need about insurance, but let me cover some basics to help you get started

Health Insurance

Most people have their health insurance through their employer and healthy people don't give it a second thought. If you're healthy, you are the one I worry about the most. Those of us over 40 and who've had a few health issues over the years appreciate that you simply cannot take the risk of being without health insurance for even one month between jobs.

If you have a major health problem during a period when you have no insurance, you could find yourself in bankruptcy. It is certainly true that in the U.S., your ability to pay will not prevent you from receiving emergency or life sustaining care, but you will be expected to pay everything you have toward that care.

An affluent friend of mine had a bout with cancer a decade ago. He still makes monthly installments of thousands of dollars to pay the bills for his treatments. He has no cushion, no savings and almost no ability to give generously to a cause today because he is so deep in the hole because he got cancer at a time when he didn't have insurance.

If you are between jobs, there is a federal law that requires your former employer to allow you to buy your old insurance at its full cost. It may be shockingly expensive, but it's cheaper by far than having a health crisis while you are uninsured. There are other options as well for those who have no employer-provided health insurance so don't make excuses, find some insurance.

Auto Insurance

Most states have efficient mechanisms for requiring car owners to have at least some minimal amount of insurance. The problem is that the state limits are far too low for anyone who now has or hopes to have any assets or income to protect. And the insurance required by the state doesn't protect your car—it protects the other cars and the passengers.

There are two primary parts to your auto policy: the liability side that protects other people from you and the comprehensive and collision insurance that protects your car.

In some states, a liability limit of $50,000 may be all that is required. That's great until you total a high end Mercedes, BMW, Cadillac, Ferrari, Porsche, Audi, or Lexus (and I'm sure I'm forgetting plenty of folks who make cars that cost more than $50,000). It is true, if you have an "at fault" accident, it is most likely to be with a more ordinary car, but it certainly could be with a much more expensive car.

The best news is that because the odds are low that you'll need to call on such extreme coverage, it doesn't cost very much. You can also save enough for this by dropping coverage you don't need. If you drive an old car, you may want to drop collision and comprehensive policies altogether—I drop those policies once my car seems to be worth less than $5,000, figuring that I'll just buy another clunker if need be. If your car is still quite valuable, you may want to consider higher deductibles. Many people choose low deductibles like $200 or $500. You may be better off taking those risks you can afford to absorb—even though they are likely to occur—in order to make your premium affordable enough to cover the losses you could never afford.

Here is what happens in the real world as a result of following this plan. You drive your car and you get a small ding or scrape that would cost about $2,000 to fix. If you have the low deductible, you'll call your agent and arrange to have the car fixed and you're back to driving a like-new car (after you pay your deductible). If you have the $2,000 deductible I recommend, you drive your car around and get a small ding or scrape that would cost about $2,000 to fix and you simply don't fix it. You drive a car with a ding. If you're going to keep your car for seven years, it's going to get some scratches along the way. Don't sweat it. Don't insure for scratches. Insure yourself against the liability of wiping out a Mercedes!

If you hit and total a $75,000 Mercedes while you are at fault—presuming no one is hurt—and you have only $50,000 of liability insurance, you will have to come up with $25,000. The cost of insuring for this risk is small, but the cost of not having the insurance if you need it is very high. Talk to your agent to be sure you have the right deductibles and the right limits on your policy.

Homeowners Insurance

When you bought your home, the lender required—among about 1,000 other things—that you buy a good homeowners insurance policy to guaranty that if the house burns down they'll get paid. (You thought it was because they were worried you wouldn't have a place to live.)

Like an auto policy, the homeowners policy also includes protection for your home and a liability policy to cover the risk of certain accidents that might occur in your home.

Homeowners policies are remarkably inexpensive when you consider the cost of the home compared to your car. It seems all out of proportion. Of course, this is because you don't drive your house around. Because a homeowners policy is so affordable, be sure to get one with the right liability limits. If a neighbor child is playing in your yard and is seriously injured or killed, you will really want to have high liability limits in that policy.

Be aware that there are some hazards that are not covered by your homeowners policy. Flood, earthquake and hurricane policies are good examples.

Be sure to get flood insurance from the National Flood Insurance Program if you are anywhere near a flood plain. It is affordable and without it you could lose everything.

Earthquake insurance is very expensive. Talk to your agent about this policy to determine if you should have it.

Hurricane policies are generally sold with a waiting period so that you don't call to buy the insurance only when you hear a storm is coming. It is a good idea to buy the policy when you buy the house, if you live in a coastal area where hurricanes are possible.

Umbrella Policy

An umbrella policy is a liability policy that sits on top of your home and auto insurance to provide additional protection.

This is worst-case scenario insurance. Take for instance that you are at fault in an accident with a minivan that kills six cub scouts. Even a $300,000 limit—a relatively big limit with an auto policy—will not cover the claims that are likely to result and again you could find yourself completely wiped out financially, just at a time when you are likely to be emotionally and perhaps physically spent as well. Of course, you can never buy enough insurance to protect you from every conceivable liability, but an umbrella policy helps give you that extra level of protection.

Umbrella policies are not very expensive because they are only triggered if your home and auto policies don't cover the full claim—these are rare events.

Umbrella policies may also provide some liability protection related to some of your work and volunteer activities. If you are sued as a result of something you did while sitting on a community board for a non-profit organization your policy may pitch in to help.

As a result, the policy may be difficult to get if you are on a corporate or non-profit board of directors. This is a reason to get the policy in place when you are young and have relatively few risks. The policy won't be cancelled if you later join a board of directors.

Life Insurance

If you have no dependents you don't need life insurance. Skip this section. Don't let a life insurance agent sell you any life insurance as an investment. Generally, you can buy similar investment products without insurance features (that you clearly don't need) that have better returns—precisely because there is no insurance feature.

For the rest of us, we need to be focusing on the needs of our dependents. As the breadwinner in the family, you'll want to thoughtfully decide with your spouse how much of your income you want to replace and for how long. Life insurance proceeds will not be taxed, so you won't need to replace your gross salary, only your after tax salary. You won't be buying any clothes or food after you're gone, so don't insure that either.

You will want to have enough insurance to provide for the tuition plan you had made for your children, as well.

Your life insurance agent can help you figure out how much insurance you need.

You'll also want to consider whether to buy life insurance with an investment feature (whole life or universal life insurance) or whether to simply buy term insurance (insurance that is dropped the moment you stop making premium payments and has no investment feature attached). There are advantages to both; the big advantage of the term life insurance is that it is so much cheaper. Talk to your agent to figure out which is best for you. In some cases, the answer will be clear: the only way to afford the coverage you need is with term insurance.

Presumably, if you have saved for a comfortable retirement and your children are all raised, there may be no need for life insurance. Savvy estate planning, however, may incorporate life insurance into the mix to increase the value of what you leave to your cause and to your family. Talk to your life insurance agent and your estate-planning attorney about this.

Finally, you may also want to buy life insurance for your stay-at-home spouse, if you have one. Generally, a stay-at-home spouse provides a host of services that will need to be outsourced in the tragic event that he or she passes away. Explore this with your spouse and your advisors as well.

Disability Insurance

You'll also want to give some consideration to disability insurance. Often offered by your employer, it will provide some insurance against your inability to work.

You are far more likely to be disabled than you are to die, but many people are not aware of this risk and therefore lack adequate disability insurance.

In the case of a permanent disability, Social Security may kick in and provide some income to qualified individuals. This will not approximate your current earned income, so an additional policy may make sense.

Your Strong Balance Sheet

Your strong financial position provides a form of insurance. There are many of life's problems that will seem small if you have a ready reserve of cash that can absorb life's little tragedies. From broken legs to broken appliances, it is nice to know there is cash in the bank that can cover these needs when they arise. Set a goal to have and keep a year's worth of cash on hand to get you through any foreseeable problem.

Of course, that strong balance sheet will also become a target if you ever have a liability arise from something you've done, so be sure to insure all the risks you should!

Chapter 21

All Sunshine and Rainbows

Visitors to China are often counseled to remember, "You can't change China." With 1.3 billion people and a recorded history of over 5,000 years, the culture has a lot of momentum. One person really can't make a difference. Trying to make a change can drive you crazy.[33]

Apparently, no one told Becky Mitchell.

Becky first came to China with her husband Ken in the fall of 2000 to teach for one year at Shandong Medical University in Jinan. They returned in 2002 to teach English at Nanjing University, staying through the spring semester of 2003 and returned home. Apparently, they left something—perhaps a piece of their hearts—in China, because they returned again to teach—this time in Beijing—for a semester in the spring of 2004.

It seems Becky still didn't feel like she'd finished what she came to do, so she returned with Ken in the fall of 2009 to teach at Nanjing University and when I met her in the Spring of 2012, she was only reluctantly acknowledging that this would likely be her last year in China.

For Becky, teaching English was an excuse to share her love of service with China. While there are innumerable kind people in China, organized volunteering is relatively new—something that began emerging in the 1980s and is

---

33 Most of the information for this story comes from a visit to Nanjing that I made in May of 2012, where I visited at length with Becky Mitchell; Aida, Liu Yan Hua; Laura, Cheng Hui; Amelia, Huang Xin Yi; Smile, Fu Cong; Aki, Chai Xiang Nan; Penny, Cao Shu Fen; John, Wang Zai Yu; Jane, Jin Jian; Hua Wei Na; and Hermione, He Wen Jun.

becoming genuinely fashionable among high school and college students in modern China, but for most people here it is something you do once or twice to say you've done it.

Back in 2002, Becky was assigned to teach some classes on a satellite campus of Nanjing University one day each week. The campus was in Pukou, across the Yangtze River from Nanjing, requiring her to travel about an hour in each direction. With both a morning and an afternoon class, she had time to fill at lunch. I can't help but think that a real English teacher would have relished this time to read each day, but as I told you, Becky is not a real English teacher. Instead, she invited her students to join her each week for "leadership training."

She was surprised when most of her students chose to participate in this optional leadership training session each week. As the semester wore on, Becky drew on her years of experience with 4-H to form her leadership group into a 4-H chapter. They decided to do two things that turned out to have an enduring impact. First, they decided to have a Christmas party, complete with a Santa Claus (played by Ken) and to raise money at the party for a to-be-defined-later program to help needy children that they would later call "The Sunshine Project."

For the party, the students built a beautifully decorated donation box with signs suggesting donations to help needy children. The students contributed about $100 as a group at the party.

During this same semester, Becky was also teaching English to faculty who participated on a volunteer basis to improve their English (which is helpful, especially for publishing academic papers). Becky became close with some of the teachers and invited them over to her apartment on Christmas Eve where the teachers saw the beautifully decorated donation box and also contributed. Three of them—later joined by a fourth faculty friend—were particularly eager to help and wanted to know what they could do to get involved.

Becky asked the four to help find a project that they could undertake using the funds they'd raised. She especially wanted to find something where she could involve the student volunteers in helping with the project, not just donating money and sending it along.

One of the teachers, Hua Wei Na, an Information Science professor, found two schools in a distant, rural suburb of Nanjing that were interested in the help from the University volunteers. Becky and Wei Na visited the two schools. At the larger of the two, the school was able to quickly articulate uses for the money, but could not articulate a need for the volunteers.

At the other school, Gao Chuan Special Education School, a much smaller and less well-funded boarding school for deaf children, they were eager to have the volunteers get involved to provide an opportunity for their children to interact with hearing people—an opportunity they rarely had. They also learned their money could be used to enroll more students at the school who couldn't otherwise attend, but who also needed the special programs it offered.

It was exactly what they had been hoping to find. Working together with the students, the four teachers and Becky organized a "Fun Field Day" to visit the little school in Gao Chuan. On that first visit, they rounded up several used computers and bought a new printer. They didn't just drop them off; they took them in and set them up, connecting them to the internet.

These were the first computers in the school. Imagine the difference it made in the lives of these students who had not had an opportunity to use a computer before and had little means of communicating with people outside the deaf community to suddenly be introduced to email, allowing them to establish relationships with anyone in the world. Immediately, relationships began to blossom between the university students and young children at the Gao Chuan school.

Since those early days nearly ten years ago, two of the students from the school, later qualified to attend a special school in Nanjing for high school and then enrolled at a university. It is hard to imagine them accomplishing that without the benefit of the computers and mentors provided by the Sunshine Project.

Every semester now for almost ten years the Sunshine Project has continued to make visits to the school and to provide money to enroll more students who cannot afford to pay on their own. Initially, the Sunshine Project funded scholarships for seven students and that has grown now to twenty, representing one out of every six of the 120 students at the special school. In addition to scholarships, they help the school with uniforms, computers, t-shirts, milk and other needs. In all, they now donate 5,000 RMB (about $750) every semester.

Even during the years back at home in the U.S., Becky has continued to stay involved, raising money and donating goods to help the Sunshine Program continue its work.

The special school has evolved over the years, too. With more government funding, they now have new facilities and a larger enrollment. In addition to students with hearing impairments, the school began enrolling students with intellectual challenges; this group has become much larger than the deaf group.

In Becky's small apartment, I met with her and the current crop of student leaders who organize the activities for the Sunshine Project. They told me about some of their feelings and experiences being involved.

Huang Xin Yi who uses the name Amelia with her English-speaking friends, has been volunteering with the group for three years. She is now the President of the 4-H club, which works actively with the Sunshine Project to keep it going. Of the students they help, she noted, "They are really lovely, and caring. When the deaf children visit Nanjing University, you cannot speak with them, but you learn a lot from them." Xin Yi will be graduating in 2012 and will be starting a graduate program in translation and interpretation in the fall at Wuhan University.

Cheng Hui, who uses the English name Laura, is an English major who has been volunteering with the Sunshine Project for several years. She will start her Masters program in Education at Harvard in the fall of 2012. Hui has built a relationship with a young boy who is intellectually challenged and who now thinks of her like a sister. He sometimes calls her just to ask one question, "When will you come back?" It saddened her to have to explain to him that she was leaving and he would have a new sister. She is proud, however, that she has been a part of an ongoing volunteer effort, noting that one-time volunteer projects are far more common in China, but offer far less benefit to both the volunteers and those they help.

Fu Cong, or Smile, has been volunteering with the Sunshine Project since 2009. She is also an English major; she will continue her study at Nanjing University next year in the Masters program in Religion. She says, "I love to play with the children. I don't just observe them, I play with them." Cong organized a campaign to provide stuffed animals for all of the children at the school for Christmas in 2011. She notes her appreciation for the leadership opportunities she's had with her involvement in the Sunshine Project.

Liu Yan Hua, or Ida, is a PhD candidate in Information Sciences who got involved when she was an undergraduate student studying with Hua Wei Na. She remembers her first visit to the school, playing with young children ranging in age from four to seven and they "didn't want us to leave."

Chai Xiang Nan, or Aki, who is in the first year of his Masters program in Sociology, observed during his visits that there really is no need for boundaries among people who are differently abled, "We are all united." He rejects the labels assigned to "normal" and "intellectually challenged" students, noting, "We are all one society."

Cao Shu Fen, Penny, who is in the first year of her Masters in Finance program, was touched by her experience with a young boy who had difficulty with his right arm. She wanted to help him with his coat, but he insisted on doing it himself. She notes, "They are strong and they inspire us."

Wang Zai Yu, John, who is now in graduate school studying Atmospheric Sciences and will enroll at George Mason University for his PhD this fall, has been volunteering with the Sunshine Project for three years. He commented on the value of the experience to him, suggesting that it has changed his life as much or more than the students they help. "The whole process is so pure," he says.

Over dinner with Becky, I met with two of the four women who have been the guiding force behind the Sunshine Project over the last ten years.

Hua Wei Na, from the Information Science department, has served as the liaison with the school since she first identified it as a candidate back in the early weeks of 2003. She has also involved her daughter, now in college, but who got involved as a middle-schooler with some of her friends. Wei Na noted that the experience has been formative for her as well.

Jin Jian, or Jane, is a law professor specializing in housing law. She, too, has been involved since Christmas Eve in 2002. She has served very effectively as the treasurer and accountant for the Sunshine Project, in addition to providing leadership continuity and passion for the project. Independent of the Sunshine Project, Jian has also sponsored two students who couldn't afford to attend the school on their own. Jian noted that she learned a lot from the teachers at the school in Gao Chuan, who demonstrated genuine love for their students. Jian has learned to love her students and they love her in return. That is a real change for a Chinese teacher who likely never had a teacher who loved her.

Gao Feng Hua and Jing Hong are the last of the "awesome foursome" as Becky calls them. Gao Feng Hua teaches Taiji Quan in the Physical Education Department. Jing Hong teaches Geology and Earth Sciences. Both are internationally recognized for their work.

Together, these four women, coordinating with Becky wherever she may be in the world, have provided the leadership and continuity to keep the Sunshine Project going for ten years, blessing hundreds of children and countless volunteers along the way.

One of the most exciting things to come from the Sunshine Project, is the inspiration it provides others to create their own service projects.

He Wen Jun, or Hermione (named for the character in the Harry Potter books), recognized that in her grandparents' hometown, a small village called He Zhuang in the Gansu Province (about 24 hours by train from Nanjing), the school there had very few resources and a great need for help. In the summer of 2011, she volunteered as a teacher there and observed that things were even worse than she had expected.

The school building itself was dangerous, featuring large cracks resulting from a 2003 earthquake. The playground consisted of an uneven dirt field with two basketball standards, one of which was broken, resting on its side where the kids would play, throwing their flat basketball through the vertical hoop. The teachers themselves had only a middle-school education.

When school started, Wen Jun got involved with the Sunshine Project and participated in the "Fun Field Day." She was inspired. She recognized that she could organize her friends from her hometown—now scattered around the country in college—who understood the plight of the school to work to make things better for the students there.

Miss Becky pledged her support and together they began fundraising, having both Halloween and Christmas parties to raise money for the new "Rainbow Project."

Wen Jun also worked with her father to get the project

officially registered with the government. She then made a visit in November of 2011 to begin organizing things for the project visit during the Chinese New Year holiday break (about six to eight weeks out of school for university students). On this visit, she met with the Education Department of the local government to ask them to do something about the terrible conditions at the school.

She reported that their initial response was negative, indicating that there are countless schools in the region in equally bad shape. She convinced them that by making one school an example, they could inspire others. She pledged the support of the Rainbow Project and the government agreed to build five new classrooms at the school; she says that as of May 2012 construction has already started.

Back at Nanjing University she raced to organize her friends there and around the country to raise money. She also got help from Becky who raised money for the project when she got home for her Christmas break. Becky also arranged for hats and mittens for the students.

In total, Wen Jun and her friends raised 10,000 RMB (about $1,500) for her winter visit. She was able to present the school with eight new computers and an internet connection to go along with the hats and mittens from America. These were the first computers the students had ever seen, let alone used.

Becky traveled with Wen Jun to see the school in June and to do even more work there. For now, Wen Jun is focusing on ways to make the Rainbow Project as permanent as the Sunshine Project, as she herself plans to continue her education in Hong Kong next year.

There is no doubt, however, that Wen Jun has already made her mark on the world, radically altering the reality facing the kids in her grandparents' home town.

Front to back: Becky Mitchell, Huang Xin Yi "Amelia," Cao Shu Fen "Penny," Fu Cong "Smile," Liu Yan Hua "Ida," Chai Xiang Nan "Aki," Cheng Hui, "Laura," Wang Zai Yu, "John." Photo by Devin Thorpe.

And Becky? Becky will return to the United States this summer knowing that China is becoming a very different place, in part because of the thousands of people she has influenced directly and indirectly as a teacher, a mentor and volunteer leader.

The Sunshine Project
Becky Mitchell
% Ft. Smiley
149 East 700 North
Logan, Utah 84321
USA
missbeckyinchina@yahoo.com
www.the-sunshine-project.org

One Bucket At A Time

When people think about leprosy in this day and age, they generally think of India, but I've learned that China has a population of people who also suffer from the ravages of this dread disease.

Leprosy attacks the nerves, preventing its victims from recognizing pain or injury, which leads to frequent wounds and infections that in turn lead to a loss of digits and even limbs.

Perhaps the greater challenge is that those who've experienced leprosy are often shunned by their communities out of misplaced fear. Victims of leprosy have generally been treated for the disease so they cannot spread it, but the nerve damage is permanent and the problems that result continue.

These poor sufferers live in relative isolation in small villages (think colonies) where they have limited interaction with the wider community. They generally live in old, one-room dwellings. The village may have one shared latrine and typically no source of hot water for bathing, as a result, residents generally don't shower during the cold winter months. Their food preparation is conducted in the same room where they sleep.

In addition to housing, the government provides each person with 300 RMB, less than $50, each month for food and incidentals.

Becky Mitchell, a professor at Nanjing University, introduced me to one of her students, Wang Yu Jia, who goes by Yoghurt with her English-speaking friends, who told me about an organization called Joy in Action that organizes university student volunteers to regularly visit and help small villages of victims of leprosy.

As a foreign visitor, I was not allowed to visit the villages. The government is apparently afraid of what I might report to the outside world. In addition to Yu Jia, I visited with four of her medical school classmates who also serve as volunteers in the work camps: Christina, Shi Ya Qin; Amy, Sun Ling Li; Sweety, Shen Li; Ding Pei Cheng.

They showed me hundreds of photos from their trips and a twenty-minute video that was produced professionally by a reporter who did a story about their service. Volunteerism is growing in popularity in China, but many people still seem to think of it as something you do once as a right of passage in your youth. That these students are maintaining an ongoing program of service makes them truly remarkable in China.

The students make three trips a year to the villages, one trip during the Chinese New Year break, another during the summer break, and a third during the National Holiday break in the fall.

The students seek to make the villagers feel like their grandparents and the villagers are thrilled to have them. Most do not have children or grandchildren.

The volunteers live together in a single room when they visit the village; a typical group includes up to twenty students who sleep on the floor in sleeping bags. Each day, the volunteers arise early and get to work, doing whatever they can. What the young volunteers lack in skill and equipment they make up for with enthusiasm.

The projects they tackle include cleaning the residences, repairing roofs, laying bricks in pathways around the village, and whatever other work they can find to be of help.

The volunteers focus much of their energy on building relationships with the residents, giving them a sense of belonging to China's broader society. Each day they take time to interact and play games with the residents.

One woman they found in one of the villages confessed to having attempted suicide three times before the volunteers started visiting her village. Now she is optimistic and looks forward to their visits—she has reason to live.

Each week concludes with a big farewell party. The volunteers prepare a relatively lavish meal and also perform a variety of acts. While the volunteers are not professional performers, they take their responsibility to create an entertaining show quite seriously. They practice songs and choreograph dance numbers to perform for their new grandparents.

Student volunteers provide a feast for the villagers afflicted by leprosy.
Courtesy of Wang Yu Jia "Yoghurt."

They also make a point to record their experiences with photos, videos and journals. The photos from the last visit are presented to the residents at the next one. Where the visits have now been occurring over a period of years, the residents are excited to get the new photos and add them to their collections, just as any grandparent would collect and display the photos of their grandchildren.

The students are presently locked in an only-in-China sort of battle with local officials who have banned the students from returning this summer. The students helped the local villagers to submit a formal request for improved housing and the local government complied, building new homes for them. The villagers, however, weren't happy with the new homes and have refused to move. The local government blamed the student volunteers (though the students vehemently deny any involvement) for leading this dissension and so banned them from returning. They are working to explain the misunderstanding to the officials so that they can return as planned.

The plan for this summer includes a project that struck me as impossibly difficult: emptying the latrine. The village relies on a single pit toilet and it is now nearly full. The volunteers plan to empty the latrine bucket by bucket in order to renew its useful life. They plan to compost what they remove so that it can eventually be used for fertilizer.

As you consider this project, it is important to remember that the medical school students who undertake the project live middle-class lifestyles that are not unlike middle-class lifestyles in the western world. They are no more familiar with sleeping 20 to a room on the floor or emptying latrines one bucket at a time than medical students from London or San Francisco would be.

The students pay all of their own expenses. They pay for their own transportation to the work camps and then contribute to a fund that is used for all of the food and other expenses needed for the project. Their example perfectly embodies the spirit of leaving a mark on the world as they selflessly devote themselves to serving the poorest people in China.[34]

Joy in Action
www.joyinaction.org
yoghurtmed@gmail.com

---

34 Most of this information was gathered in a meeting with Yoghurt, Wang Yu Jia; Christina, Shi Ya Qin; Amy, Sun Ling Li; Sweety, Shen Li; Ding Pei Cheng on May 21, 2012 in Nanjing, China on the campus of Nanjing University. Additional information was gathered via email and phone conversations.

Chapter 22

Find the Joy of Service in Retirement

As you are focused on making a difference in the world, retirement can be a special time when you engage more of your time and energy into the cause you most want to serve. Whether you do that right from your home or you travel abroad to serve, you can find retirement to be a joyful time when your lifetime of part-time service can mature into periods of full-time service.

Preparing for that time is relatively simple.

The first key is to be sure to own a home and be completely out of debt when you retire—including your mortgage. If there are no trolls in your home at all, you've maximized your ability to serve. You won't have to worry that while you're drilling wells in Africa—or caring for orphans in China—that trolls are eating you out of house and home (refer back to the chapter on debt).

You'll want to save and invest enough that you can replace a substantial part of your income with investment income. Given that retirement can last for forty years, I recommend setting an investment goal that will allow you to achieve your target lifestyle from living on less than all of your income, so your income will grow with inflation throughout retirement. This will also leave you with plenty of assets to leave to your family and your cause! Your mark on the world can be indelible!

Let's give some consideration to how much of your income you'll want to replace with investment income. Most people do have some expenses that will end when the job ends. For instance, after you stop working fulltime you may not want, or need, two cars. Your tax situation may also improve as your taxable income may be lower with some income hidden from tax in retirement accounts (more about that later). You also won't need to be earning money to save for retirement, nor will you (unless you continued adding children to your family well into your forties) be paying for college tuition for your children. Even if you do have some college expenses in the early years of your retirement, they are likely to end before you do!

During most of your retirement you can count on some Social Security income. It is unlikely to be as rich as what current retirees receive, simply because the math doesn't work. Americans live too long. Benefits will likely both start later in life and will grow more slowly than inflation, meaning that later in life our Social Security income will likely provide a smaller portion of our required income each month. Furthermore, the higher your income, the more you'll need to save proportionally because Social Security won't provide as high a proportion of your income. The good news, of course, is that those with higher incomes can afford to save more.

You and your advisors, working together, can determine how much of your income you'll need to replace. For purposes of this discussion, we'll assume that due to a combination of anticipated Social Security benefits, lower taxes and lower expenses, you will need to save enough to generate 50% of your pre-retirement income plus enough to keep that income growing roughly with inflation.

What you need to be saving each month for retirement as a percentage of your current income is really now just a function of two things: 1) how long until you want to retire and, 2) how much money you already have saved.

The following chart allows you to simply look up the percentage of your income you should save based on those two factors. Your savings is estimated only loosely in the table as a multiple of your current income. So, if you have an annual income of $100,000 and you have $50,000 saved for retirement, you'd look in the column labeled "0.5" because $50,000 is equal to 0.5 times $100,000. If you have $300,000 in retirement savings, you'd look under the column labeled "3." The table is not complete enough to cover every scenario, so use the column that is the closest to your savings multiple. If you have $300,000 saved and you have an income of $150,000 per year, your savings multiple is 2. You can easily extrapolate the savings target for your situation by taking the average of columns "1" and "3."

After determining the columns to review, you just need to look down the chart until you find the number of years to retirement. The number in the chart will give you the percentage of your monthly income you should save each month. If you really want to save enough to have 60% of your income generated through investments, just multiply the result from the table by 1.2 (multiply by 1.4 for 70% and so on). If you are sure you only need 40% of your income to be generated through investments, you can adjust the result from the table by multiplying by .8.

Retirement Savings Requirement
Multiple of Desired Income Invested Today

		0	0.5	1	3	5	7	10	12
	5	189%	183%	177%	154%	130%	107%	72%	49%
	6	154%	149%	144%	124%	104%	84%	54%	35%
	7	129%	125%	120%	103%	85%	68%	42%	25%
	8	110%	106%	103%	87%	71%	56%	33%	17%
	9	96%	92%	89%	75%	61%	47%	25%	11%
	10	84%	81%	78%	65%	52%	39%	20%	7%
	11	75%	72%	69%	57%	45%	33%	15%	3%
	12	67%	64%	62%	50%	39%	28%	11%	0%
	13	61%	58%	55%	45%	34%	24%	8%	0%
	14	55%	52%	50%	40%	30%	20%	5%	0%
	15	50%	48%	45%	36%	26%	17%	3%	0%
Years of Retirement	16	46%	44%	41%	32%	23%	14%	0%	0%
	17	42%	40%	38%	29%	20%	12%	0%	0%
	18	39%	37%	35%	26%	18%	9%	0%	0%
	19	36%	34%	32%	24%	16%	8%	0%	0%
	20	33%	31%	29%	22%	14%	6%	0%	0%
	21	31%	29%	27%	20%	12%	4%	0%	0%
	22	29%	27%	25%	18%	10%	3%	0%	0%
	23	27%	25%	23%	16%	9%	2%	0%	0%
	24	25%	23%	22%	15%	8%	1%	0%	0%
	25	24%	22%	20%	13%	6%	0%	0%	0%
	26	22%	20%	19%	12%	5%	0%	0%	0%
	27	21%	19%	17%	11%	4%	0%	0%	0%
	28	19%	18%	16%	10%	3%	0%	0%	0%
	29	18%	17%	15%	9%	2%	0%	0%	0%
	30	17%	16%	14%	8%	2%	0%	0%	0%
	35	13%	12%	10%	4%	0%	0%	0%	0%
	40	10%	9%	7%	2%	0%	0%	0%	0%

Now, a bit about the assumptions for the table: the analysis used assumed investment returns would average 7.5% and that inflation would grow at 3%. Those returns require risk-taking investments. You will not average those sorts of returns using certificates of deposit and money market accounts. If you do not tolerate risk-taking well, you and your advisors should spend time figuring out how much more money you'll need as a result. On the other hand, if you do take the risks required to earn an average of 7.5% over the years, it is entirely possible that you could lose some of the value of your investment portfolio along the way, or worse yet, right as you would like to retire. Just ask the people who were planning to retire in 2009 and 2010 who had to keep working for several years to restore their retirement savings to pre-2008 levels!

There are virtually no guarantees, but understand this. If you don't save for retirement there isn't likely to be a retirement!

What if it's too late?

It's never too late, but we need to be realistic. If you look at the chart and the savings requirement for you is over about 30%, it isn't likely possible for you to save enough to retire the way you would hope. If you still have a debt problem, go back to the chapter on debt and figure out how to quickly reduce your debt to make room in your budget for retirement savings.

Once you are debt free, apart from your mortgage, and are on track to pay off your mortgage before you retire, you are in good shape to start contributing more aggressively to your retirement savings. Even so, if you are in the upper left corner of the chart where the years to retirement are short and your existing savings are small, you simply cannot save enough in the time remaining to have your investment income provide the target percentage of your retirement income.

If you have traditionally earned about $100,000 per year, the following scenario will give you some comfort.

In order to comfortably live indefinitely on $50,000 a year (growing to cover inflation) you'd want to have almost $1.9 million in retirement savings when you retire. This plan allows you to leave more than $1.9 million to your cause and your heirs when you die, because the corpus of your account will grow each year as you spend less than it earns.

On the other hand, if your retirement will only last 20 years until you're in your mid-eighties, which would be typical, you could spend $50,000 each year (with no growth) from a beginning balance of just over $500,000, but at the end of 20 years, you'll be left with no cash. That's when, if you are still kicking, you will be especially glad you own your home. Your home can be sold and you can live off the proceeds of your home for any remaining time you have. This is hardly a doomsday scenario as you would likely be interested in moving to a smaller home or condo or perhaps even an assisted living environment by the time you are in your mid-eighties. If you want to remain in your home, you can even consider what is known as a reverse mortgage, where a lender sends you a check each month with your home as collateral so that you begin to accumulate a new mortgage (which you o your heirs pay off when you sell your home).

And remember, depending upon a variety of factors you will likely receive Social Security benefits that will begin at about $20,000 annually for you on a combined basis. That income will grow (though I predict it will not keep up with inflation) throughout your retirement.

So, if you find you cannot reach your retirement goal in the years that remain, don't panic. Work with your financial advisors to develop a savings and investment plan that will get you through retirement without undue worry. Just five years of aggressive saving can make a huge difference in the style of your retirement and your ability to serve during those years.

Chapter 23

Sometimes it Starts with Saving 25 Cents Per Week

Steven Wrigley[35] won't celebrate his 30th birthday for several years, yet he's already found himself making a huge difference in the world. Margret Ellwanger,[36] his virtual partner, is a married, German woman living in Israel and she's old enough to be his mother—don't tell her I said that!

The two have paired up to change the world. Each has started a not-for-profit organization with independent missions, but similar philosophies. Both believe their efforts should support the good things that existing organizations are doing, rather than to compete with them.

They also share a belief that they should not personally derive their income from their charitable activities. Steven, has three sources of income that allow him to spend about half the year traveling around the world working at accomplishing the mission of his organization. Margret's husband is the CEO of a Nasdaq-listed company and has accumulated sufficient resources that she can not only work without compensation, she can use her money to fund some of the programs she's leading herself.

Steven got his start as an intern for Mondoro, a furniture supplier in China, led by Anita Hummel, an American woman who has lived in Asia for nearly 30 years and who

---

35 Interview by telephone with Stephen Dee Wrigley on May 28, 2012.
36 Interview by telephone with Margret Ellwanger on June 1, 2012.

wanted Steven to help her establish an on-going charitable effort that she and her employees could perpetually support. He successfully helped set up a program to provide students with backpacks full of school supplies. In the process, he began to see how much impact a little bit of money and effort could really have in the lives of the world's poorest people.

The experience changed Steven's life. He returned to college, changed his major to accelerate graduation, and began the work of setting up his own not-for-profit, Global Outreach Alliance (GOA), that would allow him to accomplish his goals of changing the world for the better.

Steven now works a graveyard shift at a halfway house whenever he's in town, runs a green housekeeping service that contributes 10% of its income directly to GOA (though he's no longer a part of the cleaning crew) and he joined a social venture called Umoja in Kenya, that employs locals there in doing things like raising eucalyptus trees.

Margret always had service to others in her heart, but focused much of her energy during college on getting an education in physics that would allow her to build a career. After marrying, much of her energy went into raising her children; she notes, "When you have children, you are Mother Teresa in your own home." Her husband's career took off, and led them to a variety of expatriate experiences. While living in Singapore, Margret recognized her children were old enough to be fairly independent and she wanted them to see her engaged actively in doing good.

It was then that she formed her organization, forPEACE, a not-for-profit organization that would focus on alleviating poverty and preventing war.

One of her favorite projects is Tabitha, in Cambodia. She explained how the organization has already helped to lift hundreds of thousands of people out of poverty, with 31,000 families having completed their programs. Fundamentally, the Tabitha plan begins with a savings program, typically getting the poorest of the poor, the people living on the streets in rural Cambodia, to begin saving 25 cents each week—often achieved by collecting a few extra recyclables each week. The money is deposited in the Tabitha bank (a cigar box with a note pad where the depositors, often illiterate, mark an "X" for their name). After ten weeks, they have accumulated $2.50—a substantial sum. Tabitha then kicks in another 25 cents, 10% interest in ten weeks, so that the program participants are seeing a measurable return on their investment.

The $2.75 is then distributed to the participants who then have an opportunity to invest that money in a productive asset of some sort. Often, they choose to buy some chicks, which at $.50 each, gives them five chicks. In rural Cambodia, the chickens don't need to be fed; they forage for food. Because these poor chicken farmers can't afford to vaccinate them or give them hormones, the chickens are effectively free-range, organic chickens—the most valuable chickens on the market. They are then sold in the capital, Phnom Penh, at a premium, yielding $10 each—Tabitha takes no commission or fees for helping the owners to sell the chickens.

All the while, the families continue to contribute to their savings plan and continue earning 10% interest every 10 weeks. Once they can start selling the chickens, their income and savings grow. They can start investing in a garden, where they grow organic vegetables that they can both eat and sell. Eventually, families learn to raise pigs, which requires even more capital but yields high returns.

They can also afford to build a simple home.

The final stage of the program is to help the family develop a business, using the self-reliance and money management skills they've been learning. A business might be simply buying a food stand or a small motorcycle or "moto," to provide taxi services.

Over a period of seven years, a typical family transitions

from abject poverty, to living in a basic home, with a stable food supply and a business that provides a steady income. The cycle of poverty is broken as children attend school and are raised to work hard to build and save for the future, rather than merely scavenging for subsistence.

Steven met Margret in 2010 through a mutual friend who knew that they both had a similar passion for serving the poor in Cambodia.

Margret was interested in partnering with Steven because of the progress he'd already made in Kenya, where he'd led a service expedition to train people in hygiene and to kick off a scholarship program to help kids attend secondary school. She was eager to get involved in that community.

He used GOA to raise $15,000 for Tabitha. The money was used to get 1,200 young Cambodians into school. It also proved once again the impact that Steven could have in the world with relatively modest amounts of money—if it wasn't being spent to support his habit of eating food two or three times a day!

Steven and Margaret both sit on the Board of the Cambodian and International Children's Friend Organization (see chapter 7), where they not only help to care for 35 children, they are extending the reach of the remarkable Cambodian woman who runs the orphanage.

In Israel, where Margret lives full time, she and Steven partner on projects that are intended to both alleviate poverty and build bridges between the increasingly hostile Jewish and Arab communities.

Margret, 2nd from left, and Steven, far right, with women in the Negev Desert. Courtesy of Steve Wrigley.

Margret noted that coming from a country that had a holocaust, many people would say, "Never again!" Yet, in the years since, the Khmer Rouge killed millions in Cambodia and more recently we've seen genocide in Rwanda. "'Never again' didn't work," she notes, suggesting that we have to do more to prevent the kind of hatred that leads to genocide. She notes that the attitude of the Jews toward the Arabs in Israel is reminiscent of the attitude of the Germans to the Jews before the holocaust—and the feeling of the Arabs toward the Jews is just as hateful.

Their programs in Israel focus on bringing Jews and Arabs together to work on something jointly that is focused on the future, to help them begin to envision a joint future. For instance, they bring high school age kids—both Jews and Arabs—in to do environmental research, which encourages them to think about the future.

With their Peace Through Teacher Dialog (PTTD) program, they have taken educational leaders, again Jews and Arabs together, to Germany to study educational models together. Outside the context of Israel, they work together and begin to see one another's needs and perspectives.

They also bring together orchestras comprised of Jews and Arabs to get them to practice together, literally requiring them to harmonize.

Their joint effort to build lasting bonds of friendship between Arabs and Jews is one that will benefit virtually everyone on the planet as the world anxiously watches every headline from the Middle East. Margret and Steven are determined not just to watch and wait, but are on the front lines of the war against hatred and the potential for genocide.

In Kenya, GOA is now launching a savings program like Tabitha's, bringing the benefits of micro-savings to the impoverished people there.

Steven and Margret are unlikely friends, living and working half a world apart, but are united by a common desire to facilitate all of the good things people are doing in the world to build self-reliance through financial empowerment and education, and in so doing, they are leaving their marks on the world.

Global Outreach Alliance
www.theglobaloutreach.org
@globaloutreach
steve@theglobaloutreach.org

forPEACE
forPEACE.us
margret@forPEACE.us
Thomas G Harlow CPA Inc
721 Monterey St
Hollister, CA, 95023

Chapter 24
The Final Plan

You've now learned all you need to know to complete your plan and put it into action. This chapter is designed to help you do just that. You are ready to take control of your life and begin having the impact on the world that you've always wanted to have!

Remember, in chapter 6, "Budget To Empower Your Mark On The World," we talked about basic budgeting concepts. You'll need those to make your plan a reality. In this chapter, we'll focus on completing that budget, making appropriate allocations for your cause, debt service and savings.

As you work through this exercise, don't panic if you see that you can't do everything this book suggests right from the start. In all likelihood, you've got decades to do it all, so don't get frustrated if you can't operate exactly according to your target plan from the first day. In most cases, it will take only two or three years for someone who can't implement the full plan immediately to find that they can ultimately get on plan. Most employers provide at least a modest cost of living raise each year and some of your debts will get paid off, if you are disciplined, so you should gain ground each year.

Come back to this exercise every time your income changes and figure out how you'll allocate those new dollars to get closer to full implementation of your plan.

Now, let's get started.

Go to this web site to download this spreadsheet to help you build your final plan: http://bit.ly/HZXEGr. (Don't enter the period at the end; that one is there just to tell you that's the end of the sentence, like the one just to the right of this word.)

Here's a copy of the spreadsheet for your reference while you're reading the book.

Line #	Category	% of Income	$ (Dollar) Amount
	Financial Planning Worksheet		
A	Income:	100.00%	$
B	Monthly Contributions to Your Cause	10.00%	$
C	Education Savings:	%	$
D	Retirement Savings:	%	$
E	Taxes:	%	$
F	Insurance:	%	$
G	Debt Service–Excluding Auto Loan:	%	$
H	Automobile Loan/Savings Plan:	%	$
I	Subtotal—Total Commitments (Lines B - H):	%	$
K	Available for Discretionary Spending:	%	$
L	Total Savings (Lines C&D):	%	$

The spreadsheet is almost self-explanatory, but if you'll indulge me, I'll walk you through each line in hopes of helping you to organize your thoughts to put this together painlessly. Feel free to skip ahead.

On line A, enter the total monthly income from all available sources. Don't include any income you can't use, like your company's 401(k) match, interest income on your IRA, etc. This will represent 100% for purposes of the worksheet.

On line B, enter the percentage of your income you are committing to spend to support your cause each month (the dollar amount will calculate automatically).

On line C, use the tables and instructions from the chapter on funding education to determine a monthly college savings amount for each of your children, and then enter the total here. (The percentage of your income will calculate automatically.)

On line D, use the table and instructions in the chapter on planning for retirement to determine the percentage of your income you'd like to be saving in order to achieve your desired retirement income. (The dollar amount will calculate automatically.)

On line E, enter the total amount of taxes paid each month from your paychecks; if you are self employed, the amount of any quarterly estimated taxes paid (divided by three to arrive at a monthly amount). The percentage of your income will calculate automatically.

On line F, enter the total monthly amount of insurance premiums paid. Be sure to include health, dental, disability and life insurance premiums paid through deductions to your paycheck. Also add the monthly portion of any annual or semi-annual premiums paid for auto, life, umbrella or homeowners insurance—including amounts paid with your mortgage.

On line G, enter the total amount of your debt service or the monthly payments you are required to make on student loans and credit cards. Exclude any car loans or lease payments (you'll enter those on the next line).

On line H, enter the amount of your automobile loans or savings plan. If the sum of lines H and I totals more than 40% of your income you'll likely not have sufficient income to save according to your target or to give to your cause as much as you would like. By reducing your investment in transportation (cars), you may be able to make room in the budget for your cause as well as the education and retirement savings you target.

On line I, enter the sum of the line items B through H.

On line J, enter the difference between line J and line A, calculated by subtracting line J from line A. This is the money you can budget according to the instructions in the chapter on budgeting.

On line K, enter the sum or total of lines C, D and E. This represents the total amount you should be putting into longer-term savings for specific purposes: retirement savings and education.

You're On Your Way!

This is exciting. Think about it. Visualize the future. You have a plan, a specific, actionable plan to enable you to leave an indelible mark on the world, to change it, to make it better for all the people who follow you. You aren't the same person who picked up this book a few days ago. You are empowered! You have enabled your best self.

Now, go do it. Follow the plan. Guard your time like you guard your money so you can give time as generously as you give your money to your cause. Bring your family along. Bring friends along. Share your passion for your cause and help others experience the joy that comes from not only being in control of your financial life but from giving it a nobler purpose.

Whatever you thought of your job last week, I hope you love it even more this week. Your employer is no longer just paying you for your time; the company is now funding your cause. The company is your partner in your passion. Reward it with enthusiasm. If you have some discretion over the decor in your workspace, put your cause out there for your colleagues to see and to remind yourself why you're there. You no longer work just for the company—you work for a cause!

Chapter 25

How Do You Get 25,000 People Every Day to Deliver a Meal to a Friend?

Adina Baily[37] was devastated when her best friend Rachel collapsed at a Christmas Party after caroling in 2007. Rachel was rushed to a local hospital in the Shenandoah Valley where she lived and was immediately flown by helicopter to the University of Virginia Medical Center 100 miles away for treatment, where for several weeks it wasn't clear whether she would live or die. Ultimately, it would take six months for Rachel to fully recover.

Adina Baily. Courtesy of Adina Baily.

37   Interview by telephone with Adina Baily on June 1, 2012.

During that time, Adina wanted to do all she could to help. The members of the church that both women attended, Christ Presbyterian, were rallying around to provide support. Because Adina was Rachel's best friend, everyone called her. She began scheduling meals to satisfy the practical needs of the family while supplying important emotional support as well.

Sometimes when Rachel was out she would return to find 50 emails and voicemails from friends wanting to know when they could bring in a meal, often offering to provide a meal at the same time that someone else had already committed to do so. Adina was pulling her hair out trying to manage this process and more and more was feeling anxious to simply be with her dear friend and her family.

Then it hit her! There must be an easy way to put this online. She called a close friend from church, Scott Rogers,[38] who also knew and loved Rachel and her family. She asked him if he could build a simple tool to schedule meals for the family. No one was thinking past the immediate need to care for Rachel.

Scott Rogers. Courtesy of Scott Rogers.

38   Interview by telephone with Scott Rogers on May 30, 2012.

Within just a few days, Scott—a real estate agent at Coldwell Banker Funkhouser Realtors who had majored in Media Arts and Design and who had simply taught himself how to do web development—had the site up and running. Adina and Scott pointed their friends to the new site and the burden of planning meals for Rachel was virtually lifted from Adina's shoulders and she was able to immediately begin caring for and being with her dear friends.

Before Rachel was out of the hospital, Angie, another dear friend from church was diagnosed with breast cancer. Scott quickly made a few tweaks to allow the site to be used for other people, and a meal calendar for Angie was quickly filling up.

Four years and 1.1 million meals later, Scott and Adina both are reluctant to take much credit for their remarkable insight and generosity—people around the world use TakeThemaMeal.com for free and neither Adina nor Scott derive any income from it. There is a contribute button on the site that allows people to make contributions and $10 at a time they collect enough to pay a part-time customer support person and to cover the hosting costs.

Both Adina and Scott point out that their site has never cooked nor delivered a meal to anyone; before the site was up, people most often coordinated meal calendars through a church "meal ministry," and they are the ones who continue to do all of the hard work. Both are proud, however, at how easy their site makes it for a church or other organization to plan and coordinate sharing meals, allowing people to spend more time really caring for people rather than being chained to a phone for days on end.

Over the years, the number of people using the site has roughly doubled every year and today about 25,000 people use the site every day. For the first two years, Scott and Adina did virtually nothing to support the site. They offered no customer support and didn't do much to maintain the site, but after seeing the growth, both have begun devoting significant amounts of time to enhancing the site and providing customer care.

Adina noted that while the site is simple and easy to use, in the midst of a tragedy, minds are not always clear and having access to customer support can make a big difference.

About one year after the site was launched, a seven-year-old boy in Scott and Adina's town of Harrisonburg, Virginia, was playing in his yard when a stone structure fell, crushing him beneath its weight. His life was clearly in danger and the local community quickly rallied. A four-month meal schedule was quickly posted on the site and when Adina and Scott checked the calendar after 24 hours they noted every slot had already been filled.

It was tremendous evidence of the love of the community for the family. Scott and Adina also knew that absent their site, it would have been impossible to organize so many meals so quickly. The real value of their site was becoming apparent.

Later on, they observed a situation that has become something of a pattern. Susan sent an email explaining that she had used the site to organize meals for a friend for several months and loved it. Then her own husband got sick and the same friends immediately created a calendar for her own family and began bringing her meals.

When they hear these stories of how the site is making a difference in the lives of real people, Scott says, that is when it "is most meaningful for me—it isn't just web scripts."

About 60% of the site users are planning meals in sad situations, deaths, illnesses, accidents and the like. Fortunately, another 40% are for happier circumstances, primarily the arrival of new babies.

After a while, users began asking how they could use the site to organize a potluck dinner, especially for a bereavement meal where the church might prepare a meal for the family after a funeral. The original site wasn't well suited to that purpose, so Scott and Adina built PerfectPotluck.com, which allows people to organize food assignments for any community or family dinner.

Adina notes, "We never expected to become what it did, but we are glad that it did!"

Adina is a homemaker who home schools her three children and is primarily responsible for managing the customer support function for the websites.

Scott, in addition to his real estate business, also coaches his son's baseball and soccer teams. Scott continues to take responsibility for the web development of the site.

Together, these remarkable people are quietly making a difference in the lives of people that they will never meet around the world, leaving a little mark on every heart they touch.

TakeThemAMeal.com
PerfectPotluck.com
800-915-7715
adina@TakeThemAMeal.com
scott@TakeThemAMeal.com

Chapter 26

Investing

As you begin having success with your plan, you will begin to accumulate cash balances that need to be invested. Perhaps you are already in this situation.

Some, perhaps most, of your retirement assets will be in your 401(k) at work and your employer's advisors will probably help you choose investments there. You may want to review those choices after reading this chapter.

As of 2012, we are still living with the legacy of the 2008-2010 "Great Recession." One of those legacies is very low interest rates, which felt great when you took out or refinanced your mortgage, but don't feel so great when you are looking for safe returns on your investments.

The reality seems to be that unless you are an exceptional saver, there is almost as much risk in keeping your savings in the bank as there is putting it in the stock market or other "riskier" assets. Don't get me wrong; this isn't because there is a risk of loss in the bank. Rather, the risk in the bank is that your money won't grow enough. Most banks are presently offering yields of less than one percent. While that is certain to improve, the pattern over many years has made clear that the returns available on "risk free" assets simply aren't high enough to grow your money sufficiently to allow you to retire according to your plans.

This chapter is intended to help you understand more about investing so you will be more comfortable taking a moderate amount of risk with your investments and thus have a greater likelihood of reaching your financial goals. Let me be clear here, and I will reiterate this again, I do not intend for you to make risky, speculative investments or to attempt to trade financial assets as a hobby—and certainly not for a living! I hope to arm you with enough information to help you talk to your financial advisors knowledgably so that you can make wise investments for your future.

Age and Risk

Before age 40, you are in a great position to take more risk. There are lots of years ahead of you for investing, to make up for mistakes or the impact of "volatility" in the markets. (Market professionals sometimes like to refer to downward movements in the value of financial assets as volatility, even though the word literally applies to both upward and downward movements.)

After age 40, you needn't shift your assets immediately to more conservative investments, but you may wish to start putting your new investments into more conservative assets than you did before you were 40.

More and more, financial advisors seem to agree that with life spans increasing and retirement lasting longer there is a need to perpetually maintain a tolerable level of risk in your investment portfolio to be sure that there is enough opportunity for gains throughout your life. In other words, as you approach and reach retirement, it was common a generation ago to talk about reducing the risk of the portfolio to protect the principal. Today, we recognize that if you are potentially going to live in retirement for 30 or 40 years, your assets need to grow. They can only grow if you take modest and prudent amounts of risk.

If you are one who simply cannot sleep at night if there is any risk of capital loss in your portfolio, you should keep your assets only where they can't lose value—in the bank, in certificates of deposits and similar accounts. You'll also want to consider three additional steps: work more years prior to retiring to shorten retirement, save a greater portion of your income prior to retirement, and look for ways to reduce your spending during retirement.

Stocks

You are a person who is focused on helping and serving others, so I will assume that almost by definition, you are not a Wall Street banker. I'll try to explain some basics about stocks so you can have a productive conversation with an investment advisor or stockbroker if you decide to make some stock investments.

In all likelihood, you already have some stock investments, but you may not even know it. Your 401k or company pension plans are likely full of stock investments.

Stocks are units, or shares, of ownership in corporations. As a result, financial types will often say they "own" Ford, AT&T, Coca Cola or Disney. Overhearing a conversation like that might make you think the fellow is very rich if he owns all of those companies. In fact, he simply means that he owns shares of those companies. You probably do, too, so practice saying, "I own Apple".

The great thing about stocks is that you can never be required to send any money back to the company, even if the business loses money. Your liability is limited. The bad thing, however, is that the value of a stock can go to zero. Even big, wonderful, profitable companies that have been around "forever" can go bankrupt and leave you with nothing to show for your investment. Think of General Motors in the 1970's. The company was the epitome of a good investment or so it would have seemed. A generation later, the stock was worthless and the U.S. Government owned the company.

Virtually every company has stock, but many companies have stock that doesn't trade on an exchange. Most of the big companies you have heard of, however, are public and have shares that you can buy.

Stocks do tend to go up in value over time. The rate of increase for generations seemed to be fairly consistent at around 10% per year on average through about 2000. Since then, however, the rate of return has slowed so dramatically it suggests the future rate of return on U.S. based stocks may permanently follow a slower trend line.

Some stocks also pay a dividend. They distribute a portion of their profits to the shareholders (the people who own shares of stock). Today, many stocks pay higher dividends than the interest rate on cash invested in the bank—but of course, stocks are much riskier.

Bonds

A bond is a form of a promissory note that is standardized and traded on Wall Street. Bonds typically offer a rate of interest and a promise to repay the principal all in one lump sum at the end of a period of time that can be up to 30 years, or in rare cases, even more.

Bonds have often been thought of as safer than stocks because on their face, they purport to provide for a return of the invested capital plus interest. In fact, bonds can be just as risky as stocks.

The financial crisis of 2008-2010 was due in large part to the failure of the financial system to properly value bonds that were tied to poorly underwritten sub-prime mortgage loans. The improperly valued bonds were trading near their full price just months before it became clear they were in fact worthless. Michael Lewis wrote a book called The Big Short that discusses the financial crisis in amazing detail.

Both corporations and governments can issue bonds. Not all government bonds are safe, however. Standard and Poor's, the independent company that rates the credit worthiness of bonds, downgraded bonds issued by the U.S. Federal Government in 2011 from triple A to double A. Many other countries have had their debt downgraded as well. Portugal, Ireland, Greece, Spain and Italy are all infamous in financial markets for poorly performing, risky bonds.

Municipal bonds—bonds issued by state and local governments in the United States—are notoriously inconsistent. That is, bonds issued by some cities and states are perfectly sound while the bonds issued by others are likely to go into default.

Understanding the bond market is even trickier than understanding the stock market. It is wise to seek the counsel of a professional when making bond market investments.

Mutual Funds

Mutual Funds are professionally managed pools of money that are invested in stocks and bonds. The money that I suggested earlier that you had in your 401(k) that was likely invested in stocks, is actually in mutual funds inside your 401(k). It is extraordinarily rare for a 401(k) to include an investment option in individual stocks, but virtually all of them give you the opportunity to invest in mutual funds that invest in stocks. Mutual funds also invest in bonds.

Each mutual fund has an objective and most have a track record that will allow you to determine how well their actual performance compares to their objective. Many are designed simply to track a market index and are therefore called "index funds." Since relatively few funds exceed the market performance and the management fees of index funds tend to be lower than for "actively managed" funds (the funds that are not tracking the performance of an index but instead seek to "beat the market") they are a wise investment.

In the world of bond funds, there is a dizzying array of options. You can choose, corporate or government, long-term or short-term, or a variety of other combinations—many of which include some dividend paying stocks.

Mutual funds are generally a great way to own stocks and bonds.

Day Trading and Other Folly

On Wall Street there are thousands of people making fortunes every year in the stock market. Let me be clear about how they do it with one word: fees. In general, they do not make their money by investing their own dollars and earning a return on them greater than the market, rather, they invest other people's money (OPM) and charge them a fee for the privilege (some will object to my characterization of the way they share in the profits as fees, but it is just semantics). My key point is that Wall Street wizards do not make their money by investing their own capital; they make their money by managing yours and charging you a fee.

So, when you hear of billionaires on Wall Street, don't get the idea that you can sit down with your $800 laptop and your $5,000 IRA and start trading stocks and turn that money into a fortune. It won't happen.

There are lots of companies out there now that will teach you to trade like a pro. Some of them charge up to $10,000 to share all of their training with you. If you have any money left after paying those fees, ask yourself how long it will take you to make that up.

There are no shortcuts. There is no fast track to wealth. Think tortoise, not hare.

Investing Wisely

Finally, let me describe what investing wisely means. There is no need for you ever to become a stock picker. You can leave that up to a handful of mutual fund managers. You and your broker can choose a handful of funds with good track records and strategies that fit your risk tolerance. You can then arrange to make monthly purchases of more shares so that you accumulate slowly over time, large balances in each of five to ten mutual funds.

You should invest in more than one fund, to diversify the risk that one fund completely tanks. You really don't need to invest in more than ten, because each fund is already somewhat diversified. If you choose carefully, you and your broker can find five or six funds with different risks, different strategies and different expected performance so that over the long haul your total portfolio will tend to grow more steadily.

Even if you are doing everything right, sometimes your portfolio will go down in value. Don't panic. As a general rule, selling because something goes down in value is a bad idea. Don't be afraid to call your broker and talk it through. Although the U.S. stock market lost about half its value from 2007 to 2009, as I write this in the spring of 2012, that value has been completely restored.

If one of your funds is doing much better than the others, be happy that it did, but don't move extra money into that fund. Trends like that tend not to persist. Stick with the diversification strategy that you and your broker developed together.

If you follow these basic guidelines for investing, you'll put yourself in a position to live your dreams, serving others and giving generously to leave your mark on the world.

Fidelity Charitable

Fidelity Charitable Giving Account is a fund similar to a mutual fund that is a charitable foundation. When you contribute to this fund, you get a tax deduction, but you continue to control the money you've contributed to the fund. So if you have money you want to contribute or, for tax reasons, need to contribute before you know where to contribute it, you can put it in the Fidelity Charitable fund.

You can then watch the money grow in the fund, even influencing how it is invested. When you are ready to give the money to your cause, you direct Fidelity Charitable to make a grant to your charity. Of course, you don't get another tax deduction, but you don't need one—you haven't had to report any income on this money.

If you need time to determine where to put your money, which may be especially true if you have a great deal of it, this can be a simple way that would allow you to operate as if you had your own foundation—without the hassle. This could be another tool enabling you to leave your mark on the world!

Chapter 27
Learning to Make a Difference

Niu Chongran, or Adrian, got his first real taste of volunteering in China as a student last year at South China University of Technology when his teacher[39] assigned the students to form groups and do some form of volunteer work as a way to develop managerial skills and experience.

Chongran was the leader of a group of freshmen that also included Lu Xiaoliang or Dandelion, Liu Shiqin, Feng Yucheng or Jack, and Zhang Jiahui or Ana.

(Long before college, most Chinese students choose an English name to facilitate their study of English. Chinese given names are often chosen based on their meaning and may not necessarily be names in the English sense of the word. Hence, when Chinese students choose English names they don't feel constrained to use a traditional name, but may choose any English word that resonates with them by virtue of its sound or its meaning.)

The students in the class were initially bewildered by the assignment, but most ultimately caught the vision of volunteering and worked hard to plan, organize and execute a project that would leave someone or something better off.

Chongran's group decided to coordinate their efforts through the Guangzhou Volunteer Union, an only-in-China sort of organization. The GVU as it is commonly known is a government organized non-governmental organization or

---

39   I was Adrian's teacher, but this story is not about me.

GO-NGO.

Going back to the Cultural Revolution in China from 1966 to 1976, the strident form of communism practiced at the time devastated the economy and left citizens in fear of their government; no one volunteered to do community service of any sort in this environment. The idea of selfless sacrifice of time and resources for strangers and the less fortunate was inadvertently obliterated by the effort to govern the people specifically for the common good.

The government created the GVU to promote volunteering in the community in 2002; volunteering had sprung to life in the 1990s in Guangzhou, but the government hoped to accelerate the development of volunteering by providing funding to advance the cause. Their primary activity is to train people in the basic aspects of volunteering, that is, why it should be done and how one might find time to help other people.

Their focus is on helping the elderly, especially those who have no living children. Each year they help to coordinate 15,000 volunteers in making 70,000 contacts with almost 17,000 seniors either in person or by phone.

After completing a basic course in volunteering, people can opt for more advanced training that teaches them to better appreciate the needs of seniors and to learn how to assess their situation and identify opportunities to help.

The most common problem identified by the GVU among seniors is severe depression; seniors often report contemplating suicide. The effort appears to be effective; no known suicides have been reported among the seniors in the program.

In one case, Feng Xian[40] or Cherry, a Vice President of GVU with responsibility for coordinating the meetings of the Board of Directors, reported proudly that one of their volunteers had found a woman who was despondent and thinking about suicide. Not only did the program visits help

---

40   Interview in person with Feng Xian or Cherry on June 4, 2012.

to improve her mood, but as her mood improved, she joined the volunteers and is now among the most active in visiting other senior citizens.

Chongran's group got involved with the 2011 effort to make and deliver scarves to the senior citizens. Chongran and his team hoped to knit five scarves—one from each member of the group, but ultimately the boys in the group were unable to pull it off. The girls came through, each knitting a scarf (though one of the three scarves was not in the end viewed as being an acceptable gift, leaving two) to be given to seniors.

Left to right: Lu Xiaoliang "Dandelion," Feng Yucheng "Jack," Niu Chongran "Adrian," Zhang Jiahui "Ana," and Liu Shiqin (front). Photo courtesy of Niu Chongran "Adrian."

Via email, Chongran told me in his excellent English as a second language, "There's differences between weaving a scarf for senior and buying a scarf for senior, because most of us don't know how to weave the scarf and we took time to learn and weave, eventually when the scarf was finished by our own hand, we have already weaved our love inside, that's enough to inspire everyone's potential of being love."

Through the GVU, the five student volunteers identified a very elderly woman who lived with the elderly wife of her nephew, who wasn't entirely out of the picture but who did not live full time with his wife and aunt. Each of the elderly women received a scarf and a thoughtful visit from the group.

Jiahui noted afterward, "From that project, I not only knew more about life in Guangzhou but also got shocked by what the volunteers did. There were shower devices installed by volunteers also a specially made telephone for the old, buttons of which are quite big to make it easier for the old to read. By marking words like help on the button, the old lady could call for help with ease." She added a note that represents the sentiments of her group, "I think we should not only focus on the material abundance, but give them more company."

The students spent several hours with the senior ladies, having already spent countless hours learning how to knit and then knitting them beautiful scarves for them. One can only guess at the impact the visit had on the seniors, but I don't have to guess at the impact on the students.

Shiqin caught the vision of the project and how it benefits not only the seniors, but also the volunteers. She noted, "I think being a volunteer is not only helping others but also helping ourselves to grow; it's those efforts that help us realize our responsibilities to contribute to the society and provides us with a source of satisfaction and fulfillment. And I will continue to do these right things."

Chongran is organizing an ongoing effort to follow up on the project and plans to broadly recruit students to join him formally in the fall; he already has several committed. When the entering freshmen arrive on campus next fall, one of the activities will be a day for students to join clubs. One of the options will be Chongran's student club for caring for senior citizens.

Yucheng commented, "For me this is an unforgettable experience... From this I learned that we can help people and we should help people who need. I can never forget the smile in the old lady's face."[41]

Guangzhou Volunteers Union
www.gzvu.org.cn
email: gvu83936660@126.com
Community Service Center
Sixth Floor
No. 68 Central City West,
Guangzhou City, Guangdong, China

---

41 Some of the information in this story was provided by the students via email in June of 2012; additional information was gathered in person.

Chapter 28

Where To Put Your Money

In the last chapter we talked about investments, stocks, bonds and the like. In this chapter we'll cover some of the basics about the sorts of accounts you should consider using for your money.

This can be more important than how you invest your money, because the type of account you use will determine how much you pay in taxes, and what doesn't go to taxes can ultimately go to support your cause instead.

At work, I hope you are already contributing to a 401(k). The vast majority of employers now offer a 401(k), either in addition to a traditional pension plan (if you are in that declining group, count your blessings) or instead of a pension. If you are under 40, you've probably heard of pensions and understand they are something "old people" get, but you have not likely been offered one during your career.

If you are lucky enough to be entitled to a pension (a defined benefit plan), your employer is putting money away for your retirement and promises to pay you a retirement benefit according to a formula determined by your employment, not by the markets. Be sure you understand exactly how much you are likely to receive if you finish your career with this company (presuming you plan to do so) and you can reduce your retirement savings accordingly.

One word of caution, however. There is literally no guarantee that your employer will wisely invest the money that it sets aside for your retirement or that it will be adequate to fund the retirement promises made to all of the employees that are entitled to such benefits. If, as I mentioned in the last chapter, stock market returns are lower in the next 50 years than they have been in the last 50 years, many pension funds will not be able to meet the obligations associated with them without an infusion of cash from the employer. If the employer is a troubled old company or a state or municipal government, there is reason to worry that you will not get all the money promised you. Don't panic; just contribute a bit more than you otherwise might to your 401(k) or IRA. We'll talk more about those account types now.

401(k)s

A 401(k) is an account known by its section of the Internal Revenue Code. The money you contribute will be yours to keep—don't worry. If you have $100 taken out of your check and put into the 401(k), that money is yours. It may be difficult to spend until you retire (and that's really a good thing, especially if you like cars as much as I do) but the money is yours.

Many employers will also contribute to your 401(k), usually in the form of a match, where the company contributes $0.50 or $1.00 for each $1.00 you contribute. The money the company contributes for you will be treated differently than the money you contribute—in most cases. Generally, that money won't really be yours until it "vests." You become vested over time. The rules vary widely from company to company, but if the employer contribution at your company is subject to vesting (and most are) then it will likely take two to six years for the company match portion of your account to become yours. In many cases, it will "vest" in pieces sometimes called "tranches" where, say, 20% of the employer's match vests each year.

Your human resources office can help you understand how your 401(k) works if you have any questions. It is a good idea to understand this.

Generally, the company will try to help you get to the point that if you contribute all that is required to get the company match, your contribution plus the company's contribution will total about 10% of your compensation. For you young people or for those of you who have been saving money at that rate from your first job, 10% will be all you'll need to save. It is easy and virtually painless!

Here is the problem. Having worked in a position to know about this stuff, I can tell you that many employees, especially the younger ones, don't contribute enough to their 401(k) to get the full employer match. For a moment, I need to talk to you folks alone. If you contribute to your 401(k) enough to get the full employer match, skip down to the paragraph labeled "Traditional" because I'm not talking to you right now.

OK. We're alone. I don't want to embarrass you, so I asked the other people to leave. I want to look you in the eye right now and tell you that your number one priority for organizing your financial affairs is to stop walking away from free money! Your employer is just plain and simple giving you extra money, basically for nothing. You don't have to work harder. You don't have to produce more. You don't have to be any more educated. You simply have to put a few (more) dollars into a tax protected investment account that will eventually empower your vision for your cause and the company will throw some in as well. This is the easiest money you will ever get. Period. End of story. You're right; this is a conspiracy to "force" you to save for retirement. Be thankful and think of all the years you'll be able to spend serving your cause in retirement having saved wisely from your earliest years of employment!

Traditional 401(k): A traditional 401(k) is one in which your contributions grow on a tax deferred basis as long as they stay in the account (you can transfer the money to an IRA when you leave your employer, regardless of your age). The best part about this type of 401(k) is that when you make a contribution to the account, it is tax deductible. In other words, that amount of your income will be excluded from the portion on which you'll pay income tax to the IRS or your state or municipality. This makes it easier to make the contribution because it won't reduce your take home pay as much. If you live in a state where you pay a 5% tax and you are in the 28% Federal tax bracket, you'll save over 30%. In other words, if you contribute $100 to your 401(k), your cash flow will drop by less than $70. Here's the bad news. When you take money out of this account for retirement (any time after age 59 1/2), you will have to pay tax. While you may be in a lower tax bracket in retirement, tax rates may be higher (have you checked the size of the National Debt lately?). In any case, this account is a great way to accumulate savings because it is easier to make contributions and the money will grow without paying any taxes.

Roth 401(k): Your employer may or may not offer a Roth 401(k) option. A Roth 401(k) is a special 401(k) where your contributions not only grow without any taxes, they can be spent in retirement without paying any tax—ever! Imagine accumulating a million dollars in your 401(k) and then judiciously spending that money during retirement and never sending the IRS a dime! Doesn't that sound delicious! Here's the catch: the money you contribute is not tax deductible. In other words, unlike the traditional account described above, so if you contribute $100 from your paycheck into your Roth 401(k), it will cost you $100.

Roth v. Traditional 401(k) Comparison: There are a variety of arguments on both sides of the coin. Unless you know what your tax rate will be in retirement (and none of us do), you can't really know which is better. There are a couple of situations, however, where the Roth is better.

First, if you have no taxable income—that is to say you pay no tax on your income—you'll get no deduction from your contribution to the Traditional 401(k), so contribute to the Roth 401(k) instead. You might not have taxable income even if you have a job, if you have lots of children, have modest income, or if you make unusually large contributions to your cause (*you go girl!*)—or a combination of these factors.

Second, if you will max out the statutory limit on contributions to your 401(k) (the limit rises with inflation every year; for 2012 the IRS limit is $17,000) you would be better off contributing part or all of your money to the Roth 401(k). By contributing to the Roth 401(k) rather than the Traditional 401(k), you are effectively contributing more. Because the Traditional 401(k) will be taxed and the Roth 401(k) money will not be taxed during retirement, the money is worth more to you in the Roth account—as much as 50% more. So, when you are capped, you are better off contributing to the Roth 401(k).

Bottom line: talk to your employer and your 401(k) plan administrator about your options, carefully evaluate your budget and make the largest contribution you can.

Individual Retirement Arrangements (IRAs)

IRAs are also available in Traditional and Roth versions, with the same rules on taxability. Highly compensated individuals however, are not allowed to contribute to a Roth IRA.

Generally, both spouses can contribute $5,000 each to an IRA every year, even when covered by a 401(k).

You will likely have many employers during your career. Each time you leave an employer, you leave a 401(k) balance behind. The money is still yours. The risk is that if you forget about it, move a few times and change your email a time or two, and shazam, you've lost all that money! Before that happens, take your last 401(k) statement to your bank or brokerage company and they will help you set up an IRA so you can transfer the value from your old 401(k) to your IRA. Every time you leave an employer, you'll have a new 401(k) to roll into your IRA. By keeping the money all in one place, you reduce the risk of losing track of it.

If you'll forgive me, this is as good a place as any for me to insert a practical bit of financial guidance. Don't chase your money all around town. I once sat down with a couple to review their financial situation and they had money in at least twenty different accounts—including several old 401(k)s. It took months to get the money all organized into one institution where they opened several accounts: a joint investment account with no tax deferral, and an IRA for each of them. Neither had any Roth type balances, or we could have had up to two more accounts. You can quickly see that if you have a Roth and a Traditional 401(k) with several employers and your spouse does as well, it wouldn't take long for you to accumulate many accounts with small, but meaningful balances. It would be so easy to lose track of one between now and retirement!

You may be tempted by offers of high CD rates or other perks around town to take some money and invest here and there. Please think forward to your future self, the 83-year-old self who no longer drives and hates to deal with all the paperwork. Don't torture yourself and don't risk losing chunks of your retirement savings. Put all of your money in a full service institution with lots of offices around the country, someone like Charles Schwab, Fidelity Investments or, perhaps, TD Ameritrade. All of these "stockbrokers" offer bank-like access to money and all the tools to invest your money in one place. All of them can help you make investments in federally insured certificates of deposit, if you want that kind of security.

Trusts

Trusts are a special case. They represent another vehicle for holding investment assets and can be designed to help you accomplish a variety of objectives, including tax optimization and asset protection.

I'm not a trust expert. If you are interested in trusts, you'll need a trust expert—typically a lawyer. Get a good one.

Generally, I would recommend you establish a trust only when your net worth (the sum of all your assets less the sum of all your liabilities) exceeds one million dollars. At that point, it may make sense—given the significant cost to establish and maintain the trust.

There is a class of trust known as a Charitable Remainder Trust that allows you to put your assets into it for the ultimate benefit of a charity, and to draw from it up to 5% of the trust's assets each year. So, if you set up a trust with income producing assets, you can keep using the income during retirement and leave the assets to your cause. You may even be able to get a tax deduction when you contribute the assets to the trust!

So, if you are fortunate to have planned well for retirement and you have significant assets, a Charitable Remainder Trust may be the perfect vehicle for you to match your passion for your cause with your tax planning.

As we approach the end of this book, I hope you can see more clearly how you can organize your affairs to have a remarkable impact on your cause by donating time and money now and by planning your estate to continue the work you've done throughout your lifetime even after you're gone, leaving an even bigger mark on the world.

Chapter 29

The Poorest of the Poor

In India, Mother Teresa's adopted home and the place where she labored among the poorest of the poor, countless people still devote their lives to ending the poverty and disease-driven suffering that continues to afflict that land.[42]

The Smiths (see Chapter 1) were among the first to tell me about a special place near Chennai where Rising Star Outreach has a three-legged approach to reducing the misery in the leper colonies of the state of Tamil Nadu: education, medical care, and micro grants.

David Ostler, along with his wife Rachelle, the unpaid, in-country director at Rising Star took early retirement from United Health Group, where he had most recently served as the head of a division generating nearly $1 billion in annual revenue. At age 54, he was at the peak of his career and opportunity for the Dartmouth-educated executive was unlimited.[43]

David notes that he's had the opportunity to travel much of the world on business and wanted to take the chance to do something international while he and his wife had the good health to do it. He also notes that his parents are in good health so he doesn't worry about them while he's living in India.

---

42 Katheryn Spink, *Mother Teresa, An Authorized Biography*, HarperCollins, 2011.
43 Most of the information for this chapter came from an interview with David Ostler on June 5, 2012. Additional information was gathered via email.

Becky Douglas founded Rising Star Outreach (RSO) in 2002, after a visit to India where she witnessed the abject poverty and wretched conditions in which people were living. Initially, RSO provided support to other organizations operating in support of this community in India, but in 2004, RSO opened its first home and school to begin caring for and teaching children. Beginning with a class of 27, the school has grown nearly eight-fold and now serves 225 students.

The school is well known in the community. About 80% of the students come from the leper colonies. Although there are other public and private schools available to these children, many would not be in school at all but for the opportunity to attend the RSO school.[44] The other 20% of the students are from the local community, not directly associated with the leper colonies.

Given that members of the leper colonies are viewed as being among the lowest castes in society, having children from the broader community participating in the school helps to demonstrate to both communities the importance of seeing people as individuals and certainly not as members of a caste.

Every year, David reports, a few students don't return to complete their studies. Some prefer the indulgent, if impoverished, lifestyle in the colony where they are not accountable for attending school and doing homework. Others, especially the young teenage girls, are at risk of being forced into arranged marriages by their parents.

RSO operates a bare-bones, mobile medical clinic that visits nine leper colonies in Tamil Nadu. With just two doctors, three nurses and a medical assistant—often with the help of international volunteers—the clinic sees 600 patients, many of them once each week.

---

44 Rising Star Outreach, (www.risingstaroutreach.org/history)

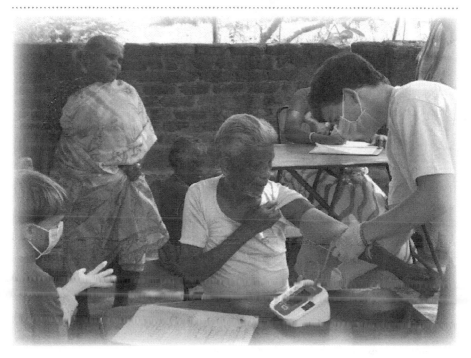

Tyler Smith (left) and Sam Smith (right) attend to leprosy patients.
Photo by Allyson Smith.

Leprosy is a malevolent disease that can ruin lives, even after the disease itself has been treated successfully. Caused by a bacteria to which about 95% of humans are naturally immune, the disease attacks susceptible Indians, killing the nerves in their extremities. A victim of leprosy, without the ability to feel a wound, may suffer a cut or even a broken bone in a finger or two and be completely unaware of it, resulting in infections and frequently the loss of the digit—if not the limb.

Long after the disease itself has been treated, the sufferer will be prone to injuries and infections that require vigilant care and treatment—a particular challenge for people whose social circumstance leaves them often without income and living in unsafe and unsanitary circumstances.

As the medical team and the volunteers visit each colony, they set up something of an improvised assembly line for treatment. The first person in the line removes the patient's bandages, the next washes the wounds with soap and water, the third treats the wounds and the surrounding area with oil to soften the skin and help it to resist infection. From there, the wounds are rebandaged.

Throughout the process, these traditionally "untouchable" people are lovingly touched by those who are viewed in India as being among the highest social station: Americans and Europeans. The patients are not treated only with medicine; they are treated with dignity in an effort not only to improve their health but also their sense of self worth. Slowly, perhaps, but inevitably the team hopes victims of leprosy will see themselves as worthy of safe shelter, nutritious food and an equal station in society.

The third leg of the RSO effort is microloans. The program operates by the RSO making grants to community councils in the leper colonies that make microloans of $15 to $20 to members of the community to buy equipment that will allow them to earn a living.

Padma Venkataraman, the daughter of India's former president and a well-regarded social activist in her own right, chairs the RSO's Indian Board and leads the micro-grant program. Now nearly a decade old, the program is beginning to manifest real community impact as there is an increasing sense of pride and independence in the RSO colonies that is not observed in colonies they've yet to reach.

Padma also created a program she calls the Perpetual Education Fund. Using the micro-grant program, community members can borrow money to send their children to school. Although school is free, students are expected to wear a uniform and provide their own study materials. The Perpetual Education Fund provides funding for 250 students each year to buy the supplies they need at the beginning of the school year and to then repay the loan during the school year so they can, if needed, borrow the money again to keep the student in school.

In so many ways, those who are engaged in making such a big difference in this little corner of the world are remarkable people. The Smith Family, completing a world tour of service; David Ostler, a successful business executive; Becky Douglas, a tireless advocate for the underprivileged; and Padma Venkataraman, a global activist, each is making a difference.

Consider for just a moment, however, and you can see how ordinary they would seem if they had not devoted themselves in some measure to this effort. But for their service, would the Smiths merit a mention in this or any other book? Had Becky done as millions before or since upon seeing the poverty in India, turned the other way, where would these colonies be today? Had the Ostlers persisted in their God-given right to pursue a prosperous livelihood for another ten or fifteen years, what would be so notable? If Padma had followed a life of leisure, which might well be seen to be her privilege, rather than a life of service, what would be her mark on the world?

All of them are remarkable for doing something great they didn't have to do, but that has made the world so much the better. When we look closely at what they've done and how they've done it, we begin to see how we could do it, too.

Rising Star Outreach
www.risingstaroutreach.org
Kadalmangalam Road
Thottanaval Village
Uthiramerur Taluk
Kancheepuram District
INDIA 603-107
Phone: 91-44-2729-2676
dostler@risingstaroutreach.org

Chapter 30

Measuring Success

Having considered all of these people who do so much good in the world and all of this financial advice intended to help you organize yourself to give more and do more, I'd like to give you some ideas about how to keep score, how to measure your success.

Let me begin by saying that the least important measure of your real success in life is your net worth. Money's only value is the good we can do with it. If your net worth is large enough to allow you to give time and energy to your cause then it is enough. So much the better if you can leave a few dollars to support your cause when you go.

As important as I think it is for you to give to your charity, what you have given should not be compared to anyone else. The only relevant measure of your giving is to compare what you have given to what you could have given. If you feel you could have given more, then give more now. It is never too late to start doing more good.

Family

There is another consideration that should be front and center. Your desires to manage money well and to give to support a cause that you are passionate about are inherently personal goals. If you are married or have children, it is vitally important that you consider all of the needs of your spouse and children.

In the end, no matter how much good you've done in the world, you will likely find yourself faced with the reality that those you love the most are most important to you. You will want to have done for them all you could and should have. My hope for you is that this book will help you find a common purpose that unifies you as a family, a shared cause you can sacrifice for together to jointly leave your mark on the world.

If that happens, if you work together with your spouse and children and other family members, your cause can be a truly unifying and up-lifting cause that binds you together. Summer vacations spent serving with your spouse and children may provide shared memories that will ultimately be more powerful as family glue than photos of the kids with Mickey Mouse.

I don't wish to suggest that you should never go to Disneyland or never have any fun, but adding elements of giving and service to your shared family experiences can bring you together in a more meaning-ful way.

Similarly, if you and your spouse do not share the same passion for your cause, I encourage you to seek common ground. Rather than defiantly carve out cash for your cause while your spouse begrudgingly watches, consider causes that may resonate more with him so you can share the experience and have it bring you together rather than becom-ing a wedge between you.

Money is an inherently difficult thing to discuss in a marriage, de-spite the vows we've taken and even the years we've spent together, we often have very different attitudes about money. It is dangerous to a relationship to think of your spouse's views about money as being "wrong." Too many people blame their spouses for their financial trou-bles because they either earn too little or spend too much.

Your spouse is more important than your cause. By working with your spouse to find a cause you can both get excited about and per-haps by starting with smaller financial contributions rather than larger ones, you can develop a joint commitment to a shared cause that fires not only your passion for the cause, but one that fires your passion for each other.

The example you leave your children may be the most important contribution you make. If they see you as committed to a cause, even if they choose a different cause, you can take pride in knowing your efforts to make the world a better place have been carried to the next generation!

Final Score

No matter how much or how little time you have left to leave your mark on the world, there is time to make a difference—a real differ-ence.

While there is great truth in the frequent refrain that you can make a difference in the world simply by offering a smile to one who needs it, I can't help but think at times that we set the bar too low for ourselves if we feel we've done our good for the day simply by offering a smile to a stranger.

Everyone has a genuine need to be loved and appreciated, but that need cannot be satisfied for long or at any depth merely with a smile. Of course we should smile constantly and universally, scattering smiles everywhere we go. But a smile won't save a child who is starving for food, won't reduce carbon emissions, rescue an abandoned pet and at best is only a fleeting bright spot in the day for someone seriously suffering.

Smile you must, but you can do much more than smile. You are among those who have committed to have a real impact. Smile while you do it. Smile when you pull out your wallet to make whatever contribution you can. Smile while you volunteer your time to advance your cause. If you choose your cause well, it will be easy to smile.

You cannot solve all of the world's problems; they are simply too great, but don't let that stop you from doing something real, something that matters. Don't give in to the temptation to do nothing, or merely a token, because you can't do everything. You can do something, something great.

Giving what you can financially and pairing that with what you can give of your time will make you incredibly powerful. You will have an impact that matters. You'll be able to measure the difference—a meaningful one—in lives saved, animals rescued, children educated, species protected, carbon emissions reduced or whatever you choose to do and measure.

Set measurable goals. Measure your progress. Make it happen.

The world is waiting for you to matter.

Note From The Author

Thank you for reading *Your Mark On The World*. I am gratified to know that so many people in this world share the vision for making the world a better place.

If you love this book, please share it. Lend your copy to a friend. Write a review where you got your copy. Tell your friends on Facebook, Goodreads or Twitter about it. Together we can change the world!

Let's connect on-line so that we can motivate each other to keep working at it, to never give up:

Read my blog and share your comments at YourMarkOnTheWorld. com. Be sure to subscribe to receive posts (one or two a week) by RSS feed or by email.

"Like" the page Facebook.com/YourMarkOnTheWorld and share your thoughts and feelings with us there—we have a rapidly growing community of like-minded people.

Follow me on twitter: @devindthorpe where we can share more ideas for making the world a better place.

You are always welcome to send me an email at devin@devinthorpe.com.

Please invite me to be your friend on Goodreads.com. Tell me about the other books you read that inspire you to be the very best version of yourself.

There is no problem so big that enough of us working together can't solve it!

Made in the USA
Charleston, SC
07 August 2012